Simpson Speaks On History

With Best Regards,
Col. Harold B Simpson

Some Other Books By Colonel Harold B. Simpson

History of Hood's Texas Brigade (Four Volumes)
Audie Murphy, American Soldier
Cry Comanche: Second U.S. Cavalry in Texas. 1855-1861
From Gaines Mill To Appomattox
Brawling Brass North And South
Red Granite For Grey Heroes
Texas In The War, 1861-1865 (Compiler)
Robert E. Lee by Davis & Stephens (Editor)
The Marshall Guards
Hill County (Texas) Trilogy

ADDRESSING THE TENTH BIENNIAL REUNION
OF HOOD'S TEXAS BRIGADE ASSOCIATION,
APRIL 19, 1986

Simpson Speaks On History

By
COLONEL
HAROLD B. SIMPSON

INTRODUCTION BY
DR. WILLIAM R. AUVENSHINE

HILL COLLEGE PRESS • HILLSBORO, TEXAS • 1986

COPYRIGHT 1986
HILL COLLEGE PRESS
HILLSBORO, TEXAS

PUBLISHED BY
HILL COLLEGE PRESS

LIBRARY OF CONGRESS CATALOG CARD NUMBER
86-82280
ISBN 0-912172-31-2
FIRST PRINTING ONE THOUSAND COPIES

COMPOSED BY
LEWAY COMPOSING SERVICE
FT. WORTH, TEXAS

PRINTED BY
DAVIS BROTHERS PRINTING COMPANY
WACO, TEXAS

BOUND BY
JOHN D. ELLIS BINDERY
DALLAS, TEXAS

TO
MY GRANDCHILDREN

AUTHOR'S PREFACE

After finishing the Armed Forces Staff College at Norfolk, Virginia in late 1954, I was assigned to Headquarters, United States Air Forces in Europe (USAFE) at Wiesbaden, Germany. As many staff officers did in those days, I wore "two hats," one as commander of the 7260th Support Squadron and the other as the Statistical Services Officer on the staff of USAFE Commander Lt. General William H. Tunner. One of the General's primary objectives as a commander in Europe was to promote good relations between the United States Armed Forces and the people of West Germany. To help carry out this aim he "strongly" encouraged the officers on his staff to accept speaking engagements from local German clubs and organizations. Given this mandate, most of the senior staff officers readily accepted the requests of German business, historical and social organizations for speakers from General Tunner's Headquarters.

Coupled with the General's request that we speak to German organizations was another of his objectives which was closely related to the first, that all officers and non-commissioned officers in his command learn at least the basics of the German language. Thus, we all attended elementary German classes for two hours a week for a six month period. The "Tunner Program" turned out to be a two way street, for the Germans, as a whole, were eager to learn more about America and the Americans and to "brush up" on their English.

It was as a participant in this program, speaking primarily on United States military history, that my public speaking career really commenced and then continued for the next thirty years until the present time. Over this period of time, I have fulfilled over 450 speaking engagements, addressing groups with as few as a dozen members to groups of several hundred. Organizations addressed have run the gamut from local women's clubs to national conventions of historical and professional organizations and included such diverse groups as garden clubs, World War II veterans organizations, genealogical societies, and medical associations. Geographically, speaking engagements have taken me to both the United Kingdom and West Germany in Europe and in the United States from New York City in the East to Midland, Texas, in the West and cities in the Mid-West including Milwaukee, Chicago, St. Louis and Kansas City and as far South as Montgomery, Alabama. However most of my public speaking appearances have been in Texas, and the subjects most requested therefore have been related to Texas military history, directly or indirectly.

My public speeches have included some seventeen titles that range in subject matter from Audie L. Murphy, the great WW II combat soldier and later movie actor, to the United States Army's bizarre experiment with camels as carriers in the Southwest, to the story of Hood's Texas Brigade of Confederate Army fame. I have selected for this anthology the six most requested speeches. Three of the speeches that have been selected, those concerning Hood's Texas Brigade, Audie Murphy, and the Second United States Cavalry in Texas, have already been the subject of books that I have written *(Hood's Texas Brigade, Lee's Grenadier Guard; Audie Murphy, American Soldier;* and *Cry Comanche).* One, the United States Army's Camel Experiment, is in the process of being prepared in book form *(Camels, Jeff Davis and Texas).* The remaining two speeches, "Lee West of the River" and "Booze in Battle and Bivouac" will probably remain as they now are, forty minute presentations.

All of the speeches appearing in this book are from thirty to forty-five minutes in duration as far as delivery time is concerned. I have learned through my public speaking experience that it is very difficult to hold the attention of the bulk of your audience if you speak over forty-five minutes, regardless of how interesting your subject is and how good a speaker you are. Too, I have found that most of my speeches have triggered questions in the minds of the audience; thus, I try to allow a short period of time for questions following the presentation. I have also learned that humor in some form is another necessary ingredient for success in public speaking. It should be introduced either into the body of the presentation or prior to the speech in the form of an anecdote that bears on the subject matter. I have always felt sorry for persons born without a sense of humor; how drab the world must be for them!

The fact that I have been fortunate enough to teach history at the college level for over twenty-five years has enabled me to practice and improve my public speaking abilities and techniques. I have estimated that in my classroom teaching career at the University of Maryland (Overseas Division), Texas Christian University and Hill College I have given an estimated 6,500 lectures on survey courses of United States history, 2,500 lectures on Texas History, 800 lectures on United States Military history, 600 lectures on the Civil War and Reconstruction and some 400 lectures on World War II. Plus hundreds of lectures on world geography, United States and Texas government and the principles of economics, other subjects that I have taught outside of the field of history.

I wish to thank several people for their help in making the publication of this anthology possible: the Board of Regents of Hill College for approving the book for publication and underwriting the project; Dr. William R. Auvenshine, President of Hill College for writing the Introduction and for his support of the Hill College Press program; LeWay Composing Company of Fort Worth, Davis Brothers Publishing Company of Waco and the Ellis Bindery of Dallas for the physical preparation of the book; Mrs. Peggy Fox and Mrs. Olene Powell for the typing of the manuscript; English professor David McCord for recommending grammatical changes; and my wife, Vera Muriel, for her constant encouragement and inspiration.

I have had fun putting this book together. I hope that you will enjoy reading it and perhaps in so doing learn a little more about United States and Texas History, which in truth can be stranger than fiction and often is.

Harold B. Simpson
September 6, 1986

INTRODUCTION

Few lecturers may speak from the breadth of experience and depth of knowledge about military history as Harold B. Simpson. He has had a distingiushed military career, having retired as Colonel from the Air Force. He is a distinguished author, having published twenty-eight books on Texas, Confederate and United States military history. He is also a distinguished educator, having taught history at the college level for more than a quarter of a century. This teaching experience coupled with his extensive military history library places Dr. Simpson in a unique position to lecture and write on military history. Here then is a book on history that is as enchanting to the historian as it is to the student. The enthusiasm of the author gives the subject a lilt so lacking in most history books. The book was written as a result of requests from colleagues, students, and friends who often asked Dr. Simpson to give them a copy of his speeches. In this new book he has taken six of his most requested speeches and compiled a most interesting and very enjoyable account of subjects from *Hood's Texas Brigade* to *Audie Murphy*, the great American combat soldier.

Dr. Simpson is in great demand throughout Texas and the Southwest as a guest lecturer. On many occasions, I have heard the Colonel, as he is affectionately called, hold an audience spellbound as he would make history come to life with his stories. His speeches are sprinkled with humor, are void of complicated words, are easily understood and are designed, not for the academic historian but rather for the history buff and the student. He is a master of the alliteration and the descriptive phrase.

At Hill College, Dr. Simpson is chairman of the Liberal Arts Division and is Director of the Hill College History Complex. The Center is a dream-come-true for the Colonel. In 1963, he started the Confederate Research Center by donating to Hill College his large private library on *The War Between the States*. The following year (1964) the Hill College Press was established and in 1965 the Audie Murphy Gun Museum. Together these three organizations form the Hill College History Complex, a unique historical grouping not found elsewhere. The Research Center, the Museum and the Press under his direction have become known throughout the world. The Research Center answers over 3000 enquiries a year from across the nation, Western Europe and Australia and the Museum and Center draw thousands of people annually to research and to visit.

Dr. Simpson, in his lectures, makes history fun. In this new book, his lectures are exciting to read and it is a privilege to commend this publication to your reading.

>Dr. William R. Auvenshine
>President, Hill College

★ ——— SIMPSON SPEAKS ON HISTORY ——— ★

TABLE OF CONTENTS

DEDICATION vii

AUTHOR'S PREFACE ix

INTRODUCTION xiii

THE AUDIE MURPHY STORY
  Combat Soldier, Movie Actor, Writer 1
HOOD'S TEXAS BRIGADE
  Lee's Dependable Expendables 19
CAMELS, JEFF DAVIS AND TEXAS
  The U.S. Army's Camel Corps 39
BOOZE IN BATTLE AND BIVOUAC
  The Drinking Problem in The Civil War 61
LEE WEST OF THE RIVER
  Robert E. Lee in Missouri, Mexico & Texas 81
THUNDER ON THE FRONTIER
  The 2nd U.S. Cavalry in Texas, 1855-1861 101

INDEX 119

ILLUSTRATIONS

SIMPSON SPEAKING ON HISTORY .... frontispiece

LT. AUDIE LEON MURPHY, 1945 .... faces page 1

HOOD'S TEXAS BRIGADE SAVING
    GENERAL LEE AT THE BATTLE
    OF THE WILDERNESS, MAY 6, 1864 .... faces page 19

UNCLE SAM'S CAMEL CORPS .... faces page 39

FOUR CLOSE FRIENDS OF JOHN
    BARLEYCORN .... faces page 61

LIEUTENANT ROBERT E. LEE
    U.S. CORPS OF ENGINEERS; 1831 .... faces page 81

UNIFORMS, 2ND U.S. CAVALRY, 1855-1861 .... faces page 101

THE AUDIE MURPHY STORY
COMBAT SOLDIER, MOVIE ACTOR, WRITER

DALLAS MORNING NEWS

1st LIEUT. AUDIE LEON MURPHY
1945

★─────────────── THE AUDIE MURPHY STORY ───────────────★

Audie Leon Murphy was one of America's greatest talents of the mid-Twentieth Century. His biography reads more like fiction than fact. Audie was perhaps America's finest combat soldier. He was the most decorated American soldier in World War II and the highest decorated combat soldier in American history. He was the author of the best selling book *To Hell and Back*, which detailed his experience during World War II and is now in its ninth printing. He wrote the lyrics to sixteen popular country-western songs, two of which made the top ten in the hit parade and were recorded by many of the top stars in the country-western field. He was a poet of much promise; unfortunately, only a few of his poems have survived. His Hollywood career spanned some twenty years. He appeared in forty-four films, playing the lead in thirty-nine of them. His was a real Horatio Alger story that could only happen in America.

Audie Murphy was born in Hunt County, Texas, on a sharecrop farm near the small community of Kingston on June 20, 1924. He was the seventh child and third son born to Emmett Berry Murphy and Josie Bell Killian. His birthplace was a square, four-room, plank-and-batten house located on the edge of a cotton field near the old Greenville-Kingston Road.

Audie had a fine military heritage; it was solid and deep-rooted in America's past. He was of Irish, English, Welsh, and "Black Dutch" stock, but his forebearers had been in America for several generations. A great, great grandfather fought for the Colonials in the American Revolution, a great-grandfather participated in the War of 1812, three great half-uncles fought in the Texas Revolution, and one great half-uncle fought in the Mexican War. He could count *at least* six forebearers in Tennessee Regiments of the Confederate Army during the Civil War; a great grandfather, three great-uncles and two great half-uncles. Three of his uncles, one of his father's brothers and two of his mother's brothers fought in World War I. Besides Audie, two of his brothers saw service in World War II. Few Americans can boast of such military background credentials. Audie Murphy was a born soldier.

The Murphy family moved several times during Audie's boyhood, but they always lived in small communities or on farms in the northwestern part of Hunt County. Celeste, Texas, is perhaps the town closest associated with Audie's early life. The Murphys lived in Celeste from 1933 to 1937, and most of his close boyhood friends were from this town. When the Murphys first moved to Celeste in 1933, they lived in a converted Katy Railroad boxcar on the south edge of town. Other Hunt County communities or towns associated with his early life are Dixon, Floyd, Greenville, Hog Eye, Lane, Quinlin, White Rock, and Farmersville in nearby Collin County.

Audie's formal education was minimal. He attended only the first five grades of elementary school, the first four years in Celeste and the fifth year in Floyd. "Little Pat," as he was called by his teachers, was a good student, but he dropped out of school at fourteen to earn his own way and to assist his family financially. After leaving school, Audie worked at several occupations. He was employed for a short time in 1938 as a carpenter's helper for a building contractor in Farmersville and then chopped cotton and corn on a farm near Floyd. In 1939-40, Audie or Leon, as he was called after he left home, worked as a clerk in a combination grocery store and gas station in Greenville. He was employed in a radio shop in Greenville as an apprentice repairman when he enlisted in the army.

For recreation and sport he hunted and fished. Audie had perfect eyesight and hearing; these faculties along with his quick reflexes and uncanny accuracy with a rifle made him a successful hunter. He could hear a squirrel moving in the highest trees. As a boy, he engaged in feats of "derring-do" from climbing water towers to wading swollen streams. According to his boyhood acquaintances, Audie was pugnacious when pressed, was loyal to his friends, was exceedingly generous, most courageous, and was a natural-born leader. These attributes were predominant throughout his life.

His father, Emmett Murphy, who had the habit of leaving home for short periods of time, left for good in late 1940. It has been assumed that he went to West Texas to look for a job in the oil fields to better support his family. Early in 1941, Audie's mother, who was destitute and sick, and her three youngest children moved to Farmersville, Collin County, Texas, to live with her eldest daughter, Mrs. Poland (Corinne) Burns. Audie's mother died in late May, 1941, at her daughter's home. Her death greatly affected Audie and he grieved for a long time afterward. His eldest sister Corinne became his guardian and was listed as the "next of kin" on his army records. Upon the death of their mother, Audie's youngest brother and two youngest sisters were placed in an orphanage near Quinlin in Hunt County.

Too young to enter the armed services when war was declared in December, 1941, Audie enlisted as soon as he was able; a few days after his eighteenth birthday. Refused by both the Marine Corps and the Paratroops because of his height and weight (he was five feet six inches and less than 120 pounds), Audie reluctantly enlisted in the Army. Although he was eighteen, with a baby face and his small size, he looked much younger, and the recruiting sergeant refused to enlist him until his sister Corinne, verified his birth date. Audie took his basic training at Camp Wolters, Texas and his advanced training at Fort George Gordon Meade, Maryland. Attempts were made while he was at Fort Meade, in deference to his young appearance, to assign him to quartermaster duty but Audie insisted on line duty. Private Murphy left from New York for overseas early in February, 1943, and arrived at Casablanca, French Morocco a few days later.

The small Texan was assigned as a replacement to Company B, 15th Infantry Regiment, Third Infantry Division, Fifth U.S. Army. He remained in this company, regiment and division for the rest of the war. Audie was fortunate in his military assignment. The 15th Infantry was one of the oldest and finest regiments in the United States Army, its history dating back to the War of 1812. The Third Division, likewise, had a fine fighting reputation. Known as "The Rock of the Marne," it had performed brilliantly in World War I and would go on to even greater fame in the Second World War. The Third Infantry Division during World War II saw more action and earned more battle honors than any other American division. It logged 531 days of combat duty and was the only American division to fight the Germans on all western fronts during the war. The "Marnemen" participated in four major amphibious invasions and in ten campaigns. During the war it suffered 34,000 casualties, more than any other American Infantry Division. Seven of the division's units earned Presidential Unit Citations. Thirty-nine of its men (including Audie) earned the Congressional Medal of Honor, and every member of the division was authorized to wear the green and red *fourragere* of the *Croix de Guerre* with Palm, France's highest unit decoration. The Rock of the Marne was the *only* American division which received this French decoration in World War II.

Probably the quality of a combat unit can best be evaluated by those against whom it fought. A few days after the war, Field-Marshal Albert Kessellring against whom the Marnemen fought on several occasions was asked by a *Chicago Tribune* reporter point blank, "What was the best American division faced by troops under your command on either the Italian or the Western fronts?" "The Field Marshal," the reporter wrote, "without hesitation named four American divisions, two infantry and two armored. The Third Infantry he placed first on his list." Such was the fame of the division to which Audie was assigned. His exploits would add to the division's reputation, uphold its honor and enhance its fame.

Audie Murphy received thirty-three awards, citations, and decorations during and for his World War II service, to become the most highly decorated combat soldier in the history of the United States. He won the two highest decorations for valor given by the United States Army — the Medal of Honor and the Distinguished Service Cross — and every other medal for valor, including two Silver Stars and two Bronze Star medals. The Distinguished Service Cross was awarded for his outstanding act of bravery near Rematuele, France, on August 15, 1944, and the Medal of Honor for his heroism near Holtzwihr, France, on January 26, 1945. He was also awarded France's highest decoration for valor — the Legion of Honor. Murphy participated in eight campaigns in the European-Mediterranean-North African Theater of Operations — Sicily, Naples-Foggia, Anzio, Rome-Arno, Southern France, Rhineland, Ardennes-Alsace and Central Europe. He also participated in the assault waves of two major amphibious operations — Sicily and Southern France. Audie received a battlefield promotion from staff sergeant to second lieutenant on October 14, 1944. He assumed command of Company B, 15th Infantry Regiment on January 25, 1945, and was promoted to first lieutenant on February 16, 1945.

Audie Murphy was not the typical combat hero as pictured in books and movies: a tall, gangling soldier, with a crew cut, a jagged scar across one cheek, a few teeth missing, a bandolier of bullets over his shoulder, hand grenades dangling from his belt in profusion, a cigarette drooping from one corner of his mouth with a smell of liquor about him and a gravelly voice. Audie did not fit this pattern in the slightest. He was small with a baby face; he did not smoke or drink; he had perfect teeth; he was soft spoken and retiring by nature; he did not walk, he glided; and he generally carried either an M-1 Carbine or a Thompson Sub-Machine Gun. After becoming an officer, he also wore a .45 Caliber Colt Pistol. Audie seldom used the Colt Automatic declaring once that the best use for "his forty-five" was to hold it in both hands in front of him when he stood guard duty so that if he fell asleep, thus releasing the heavy pistol, it would strike his feet and wake him up.

His heroics during the war included such diverse exploits as destroying tanks, stalking and killing German snipers (which incidentally Audie labeled as the most dangerous game in the world), wiping out machine gun nests and pockets of grey clad soldiers, and destroying bunkers. The action for which he was awarded the Congressional Medal of Honor was one of the most spectacular single heroic events of the war in any theater of operation.

THE AUDIE MURPHY STORY

The action took place during the Colmar Pocket Campaign, January and February, 1945, west of the Rhine River in Southeastern France. The Colmar Pocket was the only German bridgehead in Southeast France west of the Rhine River in early 1945. It was essential that this salient be held by the Germans as the spring board for a future counter attack and breakout into Southern France. Some seven German divisions defended the pocket and daily would probe the Allied line in an effort to find a weak spot to exploit and break through. Lieutenant Murphy, commanding Company B, 1st Battalion, 15th Infantry Regiment, was stationed near the southern perimeter of the Pocket on the fringe of a heavily wooded area, about one mile south of the village of Holtzwihr. The date was January 26, 1945; the ground was frozen with several inches of snow covering it. Audie's Company had but eighteen men left for duty (out of some 108) having been severely depleted by recent battle casualties and sickness. The night before, January 25, Company B, as well as the other companies of the 1st Battalion, had been subjected to a heavy German mortar barrage. One of the shells had exploded close to Audie, several fine splinters of steel striking his left leg. Being the only officer left in the Company (the previous company commander had been badly wounded two days before), Audie refused to go back to the field hospital for medical attention and using his first aid kit tended his lacerated leg. Several particles of steel from the wound remained in his leg until his death.

Early in the morning of January 26, Company B was moved to the east and took position astride the road that led south from Holtzwihr into the Riedwihr Woods along whose fringe the Company was positioned. Two tank destroyers were sent to support Company B and help secure the road. Audie was told by higher headquarters to "hold his position until re-enforcements arrived." In mid-afternoon preceded by an artillery barrage, six Tiger Tanks supported by two companies of German infantry (approximately 250 men) advanced in columns from the village fanning out as they approached the woods in an attempt to break through the American defense line.

The two tank destroyers were put out of action early. German artillery fire disabled one of the tank destroyers and set it on fire; the crew abandoned it in the middle of the road and retreated back to the woods. The second tank destroyer slid into the ditch alongside the road and because of the frozen banks could not regain the road and bring its guns to bear on the enemy. It, too, was abandoned, and its crew retreated to safety. With the enemy's tanks and infantry advancing on his position, Audie determined to try to stop the drive himself. He sent his small command back into the woods and told them to dig in and await reinforcements while he climbed on top of the burning tank destroyer to challenge the Germans. Fortunately, the .50 Cal. machine gun on the tank destroyer was in firing condition and fully loaded with several cases of ammunition piled nearby. However, the smoldering tank destroyer was a tinder box, as it was loaded with diesel fuel and ammunition. Alternately using his field telephone to call for artillery support against the steadily advancing tanks and firing the machine gun against the oncoming infantry, Audie blocked the enemy's advance. He raked the German infantrymen with machine gun fires killing dozens of them as they attempted to outflank him by advancing down the ditch near his position and by frontal assault. His deadly fire finally caused the German infantry to turn back. Without infantry support and with increasingly accurate artillery fire being brought against them, the German tanks were diverted from Company B's position and raked with small arms as well as artillery fire as they retreated across the Allied front and were finally forced back to their lines at Holtswihr.

Audie was exhausted as he slid down the side of the burning vehicle, the field telephone still in his hand. While he was firing from the tank destroyer, it was hit by another German shell, knocking the Texan to his knees and stunning him temporarily, but he was not wounded. In fact, Audie was not hit once during his ordeal under fire although his jacket had several holes in it. Witnesses estimated the action to have lasted "about an hour." However, when he was knocked down by the German fire, it had caused his leg wounds of the previous night to bleed, and his men seeing the blood on his trouser leg reported that he had been wounded. Turning his back on the battlefield, Lieutenant Murphy plodded back toward the woods. Within minutes after he had left the area, the fuel and ammunition in the tank destroyer caught fire blowing the vehicle apart.

Audie had a droll sense of humor, and at no time did this trait show itself more than during his stand at Holtzwihr. When he was directing artillery fire from the top of the tank destroyer, the artillery sergeant with whom he was communicating became a little concerned about how close the overhead fire was exploding in front of Audie. Inasmuch as the curtain of artillery fire was the only thing that kept the German tanks from overrunning Audie's position, he kept calling it closer and closer to himself. The puzzled artillery sergeant kept ringing Audie back on the field telephone asking him, "How close are the Germans now?" Unable to engage in a casual conversation as he was kept busy loading and firing the machine gun and using the field telephone to call firing data back to the support artillery, an exasperated Murphy finally replied to one of the, "How close are they now" enquiries by saying, "Sergeant, if you will just hold the phone a minute, I'll let you talk to one of the bastards." A few minutes later with Audie in the midst of calling back firing instructions, a German shell hit the tank destroyer. When the concerned artillery sergeant heard the explosion and then silence at the other end, he feared for the worst and blurted out over the phone, "Are you still alive, Lieutenant?" Murphy, momentarily stunned, after a short pause yelled back, "Momentarily, Sergeant, and what are your post-war plans?" Audie after his long ordeal on top of the tank destroyer slid down off of the smoking and smouldering vehicle onto the frozen ground. He stated in his book that "he really hated to leave the burning tank destroyer as it was the first time in a week that his feet had been warm."

During the war Audie Murphy was wounded three times. He received his first Purple Heart on September 15, 1944, while still a sergeant near Genervueville, France. Miraculously, he had not been hit until this late date, although he had already been cited a half dozen times for valor. On this day as he stood just behind the front lines directing a group of replacements to a position in the line, the area was hit by a mortar barrage. One of the shells burst right in front of Audie, between his feet. The explosion knocked him unconscious, tore the heel off of his right boot, gashed his foot and broke the stock of the ever present M-I Carbine he was carrying. When a mortar shell hits the ground, it bursts in a cone-shaped manner throwing the shower of steel splinters upward and outward. Audie, standing at the tip of the cone when it hit, caught only a few of the slivers from the explosion. Had he been a few feet or perhaps even only a few inches from the spot on which he was standing, he would have probably been killed or at least had his legs mangled. Among the five men with whom he was conversing when the shell struck, two were killed and three badly wounded.

Audie's second wound was much more serious and earned for him a fifty percent disability. On October 26, 1944, as the Fifteenth Infantry Regiment was advancing on its way through the gloomy Mortagne Forest near Les Rouges, France, Audie was struck in the right hip and buttock by a German sniper. The concealed sharpshooter had killed Murphy's radio man seconds before Audie was hit. As the Texan lay on the ground, the sniper, some thirty yards away, fired a third shot that missed him but drilled his helmet which had fallen off his head. The German did not get a fourth shot. Audie, immediately after being hit, rolled over, raised himself up from the ground on one elbow, and holding his carbine with one hand, pistol style, hit the sniper between the eyes, just below the rim of his helmet. All four shots in the exchange, which had killed two men and wounded a third, had been fired within a period of half a dozen seconds. After being hit, Audie had to wait several hours on the battlefield and at the first aid dressing station to have his wound attended to. The long wait had caused the wound to become gangrenous, and he was sent to a general hospital in Southern France to recuperate. For nearly a month Audie had daily doses of penicillin, but eventually several pounds of dead flesh had to be removed from the already small Texan. Audie spent two months in the hospital recovering from the wound. Ironically, the nine-inch scar left by the German bullet would help to identify his body after his fatal airplane crash twenty-seven years later.

Lieutenant Murphy's third wound, as noted previously, was incurred on the night of January 25, 1945, near Holtzwihr, France. This wound, which was actually numerous small punctures caused by steel splinters in his leg from an overhead burst of a mortar shell, occurred the day before he won the Congressional Medal of Honor. Thus numbered among Audie's decorations was the Purple Heart with two clusters signifying his three wounds.

When First Lieutenant Audie Murphy returned to the United States in mid-June, 1945, after almost 400 days of combat and winning every decoration for valor that his country gave, he shaved only every other day and was too young to vote. During the first few weeks after he returned to Texas, he participated in parades, reviews and welcomes of all kinds at San Antonio, Farmersville, Greenville, Dallas and other Texas cities and towns. Audie liked the military life; "it had been like a mother, father and brother" to him, he was to later write, and for a time he considered remaining in the Regular Army. He was urged by several of his commanding officers to apply for West Point and Audie gave some thought to this. Too, he considered attending Texas A & M, one of the nation's premier military schools at the time. However, a partially disabling war wound, the lack of a formal basic education, and letters from the motion picture star James Cagney decided his future course of action — Hollywood.

Audie's Hollywood career as an actor and later as a producer spanned a period of some twenty-years. He appeared in forty-four (44) motion pictures, thirty-nine (39) of which he played the starring role. Most critics agree that his best acting was in *The Red Badge of Courage* from Stephen Crane's great Civil War novel; *The*

Unforgiven with Burt Lancaster and *To Hell and Back*, Audie's autobiography. *To Hell and Back* was a big box-office hit for Universal-International, his primary studio. It was reported to have grossed fifteen million dollars, grossing the most of any Universal-International film up to that time, 1955. His last picture, *A Time For Dying*, which he produced and played a cameo role, was made in 1969 and as yet has not been released for public viewing. During his Hollywood career Audie acted with numerous stars or stars to be. Besides Burt Lancaster, he acted in films with James Stewart, Lloyd Nolan, Brian Donlevy, Jimmy Gleason, Burgess Meredith, Walter Matthau, Michael Redgrave, Broderick Crawford, George Sanders and Alan Ladd. And with Jane Wyatt, Wanda Hendrix, Anne Bancroft, Joanna Dru, Sandra Dee, Donna Reed and Audrey Hepburn.

Most of his films, however, were Class "B" Westerns. During the late 1950's and early 1960's, Audie averaged three of these a year. His movie career peaked in the mid-and late 1950's during which time he received the most fan mail of any actor or actress at Universal-International. In 1955, Audie was voted the "Outstanding Western Actor" by the nation's film exhibitors, and two years later (1957) he was voted the "Favorite Western Actor" by English movie fans.

Audie was invited to Hollywood by James Cagney, who envisioned the small Texan with the Irish name as a second James Cagney. Cagney Productions signed Audie to a contract but never used him, and after two years, Audie struck out on his own, finally signing a contract with Universal-International for whom he made most of his pictures. Following his move from Texas to California in 1945, Audie would be associated with the movie industry the rest of his life.

He was never considered an outstanding actor. He had no formal training in the field and when he arrived in Hollywood he had no prior acting experience. By acting his unassuming and natural self he won a large following of fans. Audie did his best acting in military and western films. He had no illusions as to his abilities in his postwar profession and often joked about it. After being told that the film exhibitors had voted him the outstanding western actor in 1955, he replied, "Sure, the exhibitors love me; I'm a *two bag* man! By the time I'm through shooting up all the villains, the audience has gone through two bags of popcorn each." In reference to making "cowboy movies", he said, "The faces [actors and actresses] are the same, and so is the dialogue [plot]. Only the horses changed. Some of them got old and had to be retired." In a letter to his friend, Spec McClure, after his appendectomy, Audie wrote, "My operation is still draining. If this keeps up, it may have a longer run than most of my pictures."

His love life on the West Coast revolved around two women in particular, both well known in their day. The first was a vivacious girl just off the campus of Ohio State University who had visions of stardom in "Tinsel Town." Like Audie, she was high spirited, rambunctious and quick tempered. They had agreed to make a few pictures, marry and then retire to a farm in Ohio or to a ranch in Texas and let the rest of the world go by. Although the romance was genuine enough and even torrid at times, it was not to be a long time arrangement. Young Murphy, naive to the ways of Hollywood and poor of pocket, was soon left at the starting gate. At the time of this first big Hollywood romance Audie was receiving $200 per week from Cagney Productions and an $87 monthly pension check from Uncle Sam. The girl with whom he was enamored met a man with an unlimited bank account and was a public figure of some renown. It was farewell and good luck to Audie. The man in question was Howard Hughes, the multi-millionaire, and the girl was Jean Peters.

Audie's second big romance in Hollywood concerned the starlet Wanda Hendrix. Wanda was Jean's opposite, demure, unspoiled, unsophisticated and unassuming. On the surface it appeared to be the perfect match — the handsome bemedaled war hero and the beautiful, talented, young movie actress. Hollywood press agents had a field day; they publicized the two as "America's most romantic sweethearts." Audie and Wanda were married in January, 1949; the wedding was one of the top Hollywood events of the 1948-49 winter social season. Predictably, the marriage lasted only a few months. Audie was later to comment that the only thing that the two really had in common was a love for poetry. Wanda called it quits for good when Audie scared her to death one night while they were on location for a film. The combat hero and the Dresden doll were staying at a nearby motel when Audie, in the middle of the night, had one of his many horrendous recurring nightmares and blew the night light switch out of the wall with the German Luger that he kept under his pillow. The brilliant flashes from the gun, the acrid smell of smoke, the deafening noise the firing made in a small room, and the shattering of the light switch and adjacent wall completely unnerved the nineteen-year-old starlet. She was never the same after that.

Audie's third and last major romance was with a comely Braniff Airline stewardess from Oklahoma, Pamela Archer. They were married in April, 1951, and although the road was rocky at times, the marriage survived. Pamela bore Audie two sons, Terry and Skipper, and the family still resides on the West Coast.

Audie Murphy was considered to be one of the "fastest draws" on the Hollywood scene and also one of the best horseback riders. Rod Redwing, an expert on the fast draw and probably the fastest draw in Hollywood, considered Audie the fastest man with a gun besides himself. Redwing could draw and fire in one second and was hired by several of the studios to teach their stars the art of "frontier survival." Casey Tibbs, twice world champion "All Around Cowboy," like Redwing was on the payroll of several studios to teach their actors (and actresses) the art of western horsemanship. Tibbs ranked Audie among the best five riders on the silver screen, along with the likes of Ben Johnson, Joel McCrea, Dale Robertson and James Caan.

The great combat soldier played the role of the loner in Hollywood. The Murphys did not associate with the stars and did not enter into the social life of the movie colony. Audie's loves were his children, his dogs and his horses (he raised and raced quarterhorses). He lived the simple life on the West Coast and always regarded Texas as his home and Dallas his city. At one time he owned a small ranch in North Dallas which is now a popular dining spot. Audie made frequent trips back to the Lone Star State, and it was in Texas that he found most of his happiness and had genuine friends.

It is estimated that Audie made some three million dollars in films, but when he was killed he was much in debt. The Texas farmboy was naive to the ways of Hollywood. Unscrupulous promoters and businessmen capitalized on his name. Many of his financial investments recommended by his "friends" turned out to be unprofitable with Audie holding the bag for the debts. His large investment in Libyan oil was lost when that country nationalized its oil fields. Ill advised business ventures, his compulsion for gambling and his great generosity accounted for his constant financial troubles.

Audie suffered from terrible nightmares all of his post war life. He was never sent to a rehabilitation center or given proper medical treatment prior to his release from the Army. He once remarked that the dogs trained for war were given better medical and psychological treatment than he received after the war. The police dogs that had been trained for various roles in World War II, from guarding supply dumps to carrying messages to the front lines, were sent to rehabilitation centers before their release back to civilian life. His sister Corinne remarked to me one time that shortly after the war when he was staying with them they were suddenly awakened by Audie's actions one night. He had turned on all the lights in the house and was standing up in his bed reciting in a loud voice all of the names of his friends killed at Anzio. He constantly re-lived in his dreams his battlefield actions in World War II.

Largely unknown to the general public, Audie Murphy was an accomplished writer. He had a gift with words, and those of his quotes that have been preserved in writing or handed down by his family are thought provoking as well as humorous. Audie had a sort of Will Rogers homeyness and a down-to-earth philosophy. He wrote poetry and lyrics for County and Western songs and besides his best selling autobiography, *To Hell and Back*, he wrote numerous speeches and short articles. *To Hell and Back*, which is primarily the story of his World War II experiences, is now in its ninth printing and has been published in a paper back edition, now in its third printing. As noted previously, his book was the basis for an epic World War II combat film by the same name.

Unfortunately, little of his poetry has survived; appropriately, however, one of his verses is inscribed on the war memorial at Farmersville, Texas. Only four of his poems have survived, although according to his West Coast friend Spec McClure, Audie wrote dozens of verses during his early days in Hollywood. They were scribbled on scraps of papers and all but three during this period were wadded up and consigned to the wastebasket. Fortunately, McClure saved a few of them. One of Audie's early poems, "On Anzio," appears in his book, and another written much later in life, "Dusty Old Helmet, Rusty Old Gun," I shall quote in closing my presentation, and you can judge for yourself his talent as a poet.

In conjunction with country-western song writer Scott Turner of Nashville, Audie wrote the lyrics to sixteen (16) songs. Most of the songs were written in the middle 1960's when Audie's movie career had started to wane. Two of these songs made the top ten on the National Hit Parade, and several of the songs were recorded by the top country-westeren singers. The two songs to make the "Top Ten" were "Shutters and Boards" and "When the Wind Blows in Chicago." Both of these songs were recorded by some sixty (60) artists including such stars as Jerry Wallace, Dean Martin, Jimmy Dean, Roy Clark and Theresa Brewer as well as several well known European musicians. In 1970 Charley Pride recorded "Was It All Worth Waiting For," the last song for which Audie wrote the lyrics.

In his speaking and writing Audie produced many memorable comments on a variety of subjects. On speaking about *FEAR*, he said, "I was scared before every battle. The old instinct of self preservation is a pretty basic thing, but while the action was going on some part of my mind shut off and my training and discipline took over. I did what I had to do." On *BRAVERY*, he once wrote, "Loyalty to your comrades, when you come down to it, has more to do with bravery in battle than even patriotism does. You may want to be brave, but your spirit can desert you when things really get rough. Only you find you can't let your comrades down and in a pinch they cannot let you down either." Audie left several thought provoking comments on the subject of *WAR*. "War," he said, "is like a giant pack rat; it takes something from you and it leaves something behind in its stead. It burned me out in some ways," he added, "so that I now feel like an old man [at thirty one], but still sometimes act like a dumb kid. It made me grow up fast." In another speech he said, "War taught me how to get along with people, not to be selfish. War is a pretty good course in public relations." He spoke on the general subject of *ARMY* AND *SOLDIERING* on many occasions, once saying, "I have to admit I love the damned army. It was father, mother, brother to me for four years. It made me somebody, gave me self respect," and added, "I was proud of being a tough soldier."

The Texan's speeches were well written and inspiring, most of them were concerned with patriotic themes. He was selective as to his speaking engagements and his audiences. He preferred to speak on national holidays such as Memorial Day, Flag Day, the Fourth of July and Armistice Day (or Veterans Day) and to veterans groups or to school children, and old friends he always accommodated. His last recorded major address was given on July 20, 1968, at the dedication of the Alabama War Memorial at Montgomery, Alabama. The Memorial was dedicated to the Alabamians who had been killed in World War II. The money for the monument had been raised by contributions from 90,000 school children of Alabama. It was a very moving speech, probably Audie's best. All of the ingredients were there that pleased Audie and perhaps inspired him to be at his best. The project had been sponsored by the Alabama Department of the American Legion; the monument had been paid for by the school children of Alabama; and the occasion was to pay homage to the hundreds of Alabama soldiers killed in World War II.

When the Korean War broke out in 1950, Audie, a devout patriot and still vitally interested in military affairs, volunteered his service to the Texas National Guard. General Miller Ainsworth, Commander of the 36th Division, the famous "T-Patch" Division of WW II, offered Audie a captaincy in his division, and the budding actor accepted it. Audie expected the 36th Division to be called up for the Korean conflict and told his friends that when he fought in the next war "he wanted to fight with a Texas outfit." Although he was making films in Hollywood, Audie attended summer training sessions at Fort Hood with the Texas Guard during the Korean War (1950-1953) and was involved in several nation-wide recruiting programs. Ainsworth's division was never called to active duty, but Audie would have been in the front lines if it had of been federalized. General Ainsworth had particularly wanted Audie to join the Texas National Guard to help recruit young Texans and to provide an example for other Guardsman.

Murphy's assignment during the summer camp sessions was the officer in charge of the "Bayonet and Grenade Training Course," two areas where Audie was most proficient. He had once stated that "proficiency with the bayonet gives a man courage." Several officers who served with Audie during this period told me that he had a split personality. When not instructing the course, he was a humble, soft spoken, almost retiring type of individual, but once on the course facing the trainees with a rifle and bayonet in his hand he was a "tiger let loose." His whole countenance and personality changed and he was like a different person entirely. Even after a half dozen years he had not lost his aggressiveness and his skill with weapons. After a seven year stint with the 36th Division (1950-1957) Captain Audie Murphy became an inactive member of the Army National Guard. However, in 1966, he transferred to the United States Army Reserve and was promoted to major, the rank he held at the time of his death.

Audie was killed on Friday, May 29, 1971, on the eve of Memorial Day weekend. In company with several businessmen from Colorado, he was on his way to Virginia to look into a business venture, an investment that he had hoped would help ease his financial plight. He was seeking a means to help pay back the debts that he owed his friends. His fatal flight began early on the morning of May 29 at the Peachtree-DeKalb Airport in Atlanta, Georgia, with destination Martinsville, Virginia. The blue and white chartered twin-engine Aero Commander never reached Martinsville. The pilot ran into a severe thunder and hail storm in the vicinity of Roanoke, Virginia and struck Brush Mountain some 300 feet from the top, near New Castle, Virginia. His death, as well as those of the other four passengers and the pilot, was instantaneous. He was killed on what would have been his mother's 79th birthday. The bodies of the crash victims were not recovered until May 30, Memorial Day, 1971.

Tributes and condolences poured in from all parts of the country. They came from the President of the United States, from Senators and Representatives, from high ranking officers and from ex-G.I.'s.

★────────── THE AUDIE MURPHY STORY ──────────★

After a brief ceremony in Los Angeles, Audie's body was flown to Washington, D.C., for burial. The Texas farm boy, who had captured the hearts and souls of the American public with his battlefield exploits, his humility and his patriotism, was buried with full military honors near the Tomb of the Unknown Soldiers at Arlington National Cemetery on June 7, 1971. Ironically, one of his later films was entitled, *Six Black Horses*, the title taken from six black horses pulling a hearse in a Western film. The caisson on which Audie's flag draped casket was carried to Arlington Cemetery was pulled by "Six Black Horses." A flagstone walk has been laid from Memorial Drive to Audie's grave, and a post and chain fence placed around the walk and gravesite to provide a viewing platform for visitors. The Tomb of the Unknown Soldiers and the graves of President John F. Kennedy, his brother Robert Kennedy, and Audie Murphy are the four most visited sites in the Arlington National Cemetery.

About 400 mourners gathered under the great oaks to pay their last respects to Audie. The President of the United States was represented by General William C. Westmoreland, Army Chief of Staff, the Honorable George Bush (now vice president of the United States), Ambassador-at-Large to the United Nations, and Lieutenant-Colonel Vernon Coffee, the President's army aide. Coffee placed a presidential wreath of red, white and blue carnations near the grave site. Some forty veterans of Audie's WW II division, the Third Infantry, were present. Audie's grave was under a large black oak tree just west of the amphitheater of the Tomb of the Unknown Soldier, near Memorial Drive.

The officiating chaplain at the burial was Colonel Porter Brooks, U.S. Army. His eulogy mentioned Audie Murphy only once, "Remember they servant Audie, O Lord." Preceding the chaplain's remarks, the band played two numbers, "All Hail the Power of Jesus' Name" and "America the Beautiful." Following Brooks' eulogy, as the flag was being taken from the casket and presented to the widow, the first of three volleys of firing commenced. Then came taps as the casket was being lowered to its final resting place, the sound of the notes of the lone bugle echoing among the hills of white crosses and through the large oaks filtered by a bright morning sun. When the last volley had been fired, and the flag folded and presented, and taps had been sounded, the strains of "Dogface Soldier," the marching song of the Third Infantry Division, could be heard as the band marched away down Memorial Drive. Audie would have liked that. If there was ever a dog-face soldier, it was Audie Murphy!

Audie Murphy, born in poverty, educated only through the fifth grade, and an orphan, owed his country little, yet he gave his country everything. His unselfish dedication and devotion to duty for the cause of freedom should be an example to young Americans for countless generations to come.

In ending my presentation, I would like to quote the last few lines of Audie's speech at the dedication of the Alabama Veterans Memorial at Montgomery on July 20, 1968. I now quote Audie:

> In closing let me indulge in a brief sentimental reminiscence. I open my heart to show how strongly one man feels about freedom . . . What a precious thing it is to me. I'm sure most of you will agree with my sentiments. A few days ago I was poking through some junk that had been gathering dust in my attic and I came across a couple of objects that inspired me to compose a short poem. I'd like to share it with you.
>
> Dusty old helmet, rusty old gun
> They sit in the corner and wait,
> Two souvenirs of the Second World War,
> That have witnessed the time and the hate.
>
> Mute witness to a time of much trouble,
> Where kill or be killed was the law.
> Were these implements used with high honor?
> What was the glory they saw.
>
> Many times I've wanted to ask them
> And now that we are here all alone,
> Relics all three of that long ago war,
> Where has freedom gone?
>
> Freedom flies in your heart like an eagle,
> Let it soar with the winds high above,
> Among the spirits of the soldiers now sleeping,
> Guard it with care and with love.
>
> I salute my old friends in the corner,
> I agree with all they have said
> And if the moment of truth comes tomorrow
> I'll be free or, by God, I'll be dead.

HOOD'S TEXAS BRIGADE
LEE'S DEPENDABLE EXPENDABLES

COURTESY OF DR. G. L. McGREGOR

SOLDIERS OF HOOD'S TEXAS BRIGADE STOPPING GENERAL LEE'S
HORSE "TRAVELLER" AT THE BATTLE OF THE WILDERNESS,
MAY 6, 1864.

PAINTING BY TEXAS HISTORICAL ARTIST,
HARRY A. McARDLE

HOOD'S TEXAS BRIGADE

This is a biographical sketch of one of the greatest fighting units ever organized on the North American Continent — it is known in history as Hood's Texas Brigade and it fought for Robert E. Lee in the Army of Northern Virginia in the American Civil War.

Hood's Texas Brigade, as the name implies, was composed primarily of Texans — the 1st, 4th and 5th Texas Volunteer Infantry Regiments — but did include, at various times during the War, a regiment of Georgians (the 18th) a regiment of Arkansans (the 3rd) and a regiment of South Carolinians (the infantry companies of Hampton's Legion). Up to and including the Battle of Gettysburg this famed Brigade was supported by a hot-firing North Carolina Battery of six guns commanded by a rotund Irishman, Captain James Reilly.

During my research I have found over thirty poems dedicated to the exploits of this Brigade. I personally know of no other military unit that has been so profusely honored by the poet. I think that the one verse in all of these poems that most typifies the role that the Brigade played in the war is the one that goes like this:

> We lead the charge on many a field,
> Were first in many a fray,
> And turned the bloody battle tide,
> On many a gloomy day.

Of all the military units that Texas contributed to the Confederate cause, no other held a place in the hearts of the Texans as did this Brigade. I believe that four reasons can be given for this. First, the thirty-two Texas companies that were in the Brigade were recruited from twenty-six counties, thus representing a great many Lone Star communities; hence, interest in this military unit was state-wide. Second, this group of soldiers were the only Texans who fought in the Army of Northern Virginia under the indomitable Robert E. Lee, a legendary army under a legendary leader. Third, Hood's Texas Brigade compiled a fantastic war record and these successes were accomplished under the most adverse conditions, so to the Texans back home every man in this brigade was a hero. And fourth, the Brigade was a one hundred percent volunteer unit; they were the first men in their respective communities to volunteer for duty in an active theater, and they were the first Texas troops to reach a major theater of operations. Hence, the great esteem with which this fighting force was regarded in the Lone Star State and in the South.

Most of the companies that formed the Texas Regiments of Hood's Brigade had been organized originally as local county or town militia

19

companies in 1860 or in 1861. Except in one or two cases, each of these companies possessed a locally designated, fancy nickname. In some cases these names were designed to instill pride in a particular locality, such as the "Navarro Rifles" and the "Crockett Southrons"; in other cases the prowess of the local unit was emphasized, as in names like the "Leon Hunters," the "Texas Invincibles" and the "Five Shooters." However, once the companies arrived in Virginia, their fancy local labels were exchanged for the drab, alphabetical, army designations. Hence, the game, gallant and glamorous "Knights of Guadalupe County" became plain Company "D," Fourth Texas Infantry Regiment, and by this homey designation it was known through the war. All of the other Texas Companies made this same unromantic transition.

Several of the Texans who had enlisted in the companies of Hood's Brigade had interesting names. The First Texas appeared to have more than its share of unusual given, last and nicknames. Company "A" boasted of an "Argylle Campbell", a "Winkfield Shropshire" and a "Glen Drumgoole" all good Scots; Company F had the three Chance Brothers — "Doc," "Zeke" and "Dan"; while the Reagan Guards (Company G) featured a "Smith Bottoms," a "Jasper Stalcup" and a "Elbert E. Pugh." Company "H" listed on its muster roll "Romulus T. Rhome," "George Washington Culpepper," "John Steincipher" and "Ignatz Honingsburger." While Company M carried on its rolls "Reason Hutto," "Bolewar J. Capps," "J. Pink O'-Rear" and three privates whose names would have made Damon Runyon smile: "Buttons" Evans, "Mutt" Morgan and "Shady" Roach.

The Texas Brigade was formally organized on or about November 1, 1861, at Dumfries, Virginia, near the present site of the famous Quantico Marine Base. Soon after this date (November 1, 1861), the 18th Georgia Volunteer Infantry Regiment joined the three Texas Regiments to complete the Brigade organization. The 18th Georgia fought with the Texas Brigade through the bitter battles of the summer of 1862, but was reassigned to a Georgia Brigade (Cobb's) during the re-organization of Lee's Army the latter part of that year. The eight infantry companies of Hampton's South Carolina Legion were assigned to the Texas Brigade after the Battle of Seven Pines on June 2, 1862. Like the 18th Georgia, Hampton's Legion fought with the Texans through the bloody summer of 1862, and when the Army was reorganized, the Legion was assigned to a South Carolina Brigade (Jenkins'). Thus, Hood's Texas Brigade in the Fall of 1862 was left with but three regiments, one short of authorized brigade strength. This situation was soon rectified, however, when the Lone

"Razorback" Regiment now fighting in the Eastern Theater, the 3rd Arkansas, was assigned to the Texas Brigade. The 3rd Arkansas plus the three Texas Regiments would remain brigaded together until the final curtain at Appomattox. Naturally, it didn't take the Arkansans long to refer to themselves as "the 3rd Texas"; it was probably a case of self defense.

How good was the Texas Brigade? An evaluation of its service to Lee and the Confederacy and its efficiency as a combat unit has been recorded for posterity by both contemporary and present day observers and writers.

In a letter to Senator Wigfall of Texas, following the Battle of Antietam, Lee wrote,

> I have not heard from you with regard to the new Texas Regiments which you promised to raise for the Army. I need them very much. I rely upon those we have in all our tight places and fear I have to call upon them too often. They have fought grandly and nobly and we must have more of them. With a few more regiments such as Hood has now, as an example of daring and bravery, I would feel more confident of the coming campaigns.

On still another occasion the great Southern leader had an opportunity to praise the Texans. While reviewing his army in the presence of Colonel Garnet J. Wolseley (later a Field Marshall) — an observer from the British Army, who chanced to remark how ragged the seats of the pants of the Texas Brigade were Lee quickly retorted, "Never mind their raggedness, Colonel, the enemy never sees the backs of my Texans." Lee was impressed with the fighting ability of his Texans.

John H. Reagan, a man greatly esteemed throughout the South who served as Postmaster-General of the Confederacy and after the War as a legislator and senator from Texas and finally as the State's first Railroad Commissioner, was generous with his praise for the Texas Brigade. Said Reagan,

> I would rather been able to say that I had been a worthy member of Hood's Texas Brigade than to have enjoyed all the honors which have been bestowed on me. I doubt if there has ever been a brigade or other military organization in the history of the world, that equalled it in the heroic valor and self sacrificing of its members and in the brilliancy of its service.

In 1862, when writing to his wife, General Dorsey Pender remarked, "I have North Carolina troops and am determined that if any effort of mine can do it, this Brigade shall be second to none, but Hood's Texas boys. He [Hood] has the best material on the continent without a doubt."

John Bell Hood, the eighth and last Confederate Officer to be promoted to full general rank, who commanded the Brigade for some

six months, was profuse in his praise for his old command. Writing his memoirs after the War, Hood remarked,
> .... in almost every battle in Virginia, it [referring to his old Brigade] bore a conspicuous part . . . if a ditch was to be leaped, or a fortified position to be carried, General Lee knew no better troops upon which to rely. In truth, its signal achievements in the War of Secession have never been surpassed in the history of nations.

Outstanding modern day writers such as Bruce Catton, Ben Ames Williams and Douglas Southall Freeman, after almost a hundred years in retrospect, have echoed these same sentiments. Catton recently referred to the Texas Brigade as "The Grenadier Guard of the Confederacy" and said that the troops of Hood's Division were considered to be "the hardest fighters in all of Lee's Army." Williams called the Texas Brigade the "greatest single fighting unit in Lee's Army." And, Freeman, the dean of all Confederate historians, remarked that the Brigade was "man for man, perhaps the best combat troops in the Army."

I had the privilege of representing Governor John Connally and the State of Texas at the Centennial Celebration of the Battle of Gettysburg on July 1, 1963. The official centennial ceremony of the battle was held in front of the Eternal Flame Monument, near to where the fighting took place on the first day of that momentous struggle. I was seated on the first row proudly displaying the official badge giving my name and state. As luck would have it, George Gordon Meade III sat on my left and Robert E. Lee IV was seated on my right. Young Meade spent most of the time during the pre-ceremony activities speaking to the person or persons on his left while I was engaged in conversation with young Lee. Upon noticing my Texas badge, he reminded me that it had been passed down from one generation of Lee's to the next the fact that the General had greatly admired the fighting ability of "his" Texas Troops. "And," he added, "just before I came out to the ceremony this afternoon, I received a call from San Francisco [his home] that Robert E. Lee V had just been born. Thus, I can assure you, Colonel," Robert E. Lee IV said, "that another generation of Lee's will be informed of their great-grandfather's admiration for *his* Texans."

The Texas Brigade was blessed with many types and qualities of commanders. Fortunately the great majority of these commanders were good leaders who looked after the welfare of their troops and performed well in combat.

Probably the most ineffective commander of the Brigade was their first one, Louis T. Wigfall, a man whom Sam Houston referred to as

"Wiggletail." The bombastic and flamboyant Wigfall fortunately never had to lead the Texans in battle. Everytime the wind rustled through the trees, the jumpy Wigfall imagined the Yanks were attacking in force. These hallucinations caused by his vivid imagination liberally saturated with hard cider, which he maintained conveniently jugged at the foot of his cot, kept the Brigade constantly on pins and needles throughout the fall and winter of 1861-1862. To the Brigade's good fortune Wigfall was selected by the State Legislature early in 1862 to represent Texas in the Confederate Senate. He was replaced by the best known of the Brigade commanders — John Bell Hood.

At first the Texans were a bit wary of having a West Pointer as their brigade commander. After all, they were from the Southwestern frontier and were not particularly fond of strict discipline and military regimentation. However, Hood had proven that he could handle and get along with Texans while commander of the 4th Texas Infantry Regiment, and the Brigade grew to admire and respect this tawny-bearded giant. Hood led the Texans to their first great success in the East, the Battle of Gaines' Mill (June 27, 1862), and he was the idol of the Texans until his untimely death from yellow fever in New Orleans in 1879. This Hood-Texas team was one of the best combinations that the Confederacy fielded. It was a team welded together by mutual respect, complete trust and genuine admiration. Although Hood actually commanded the Brigade less than six months, his character and pugnacity were indelibly impressed upon it and the Brigade carried his name throughout the War and even after the War as a veteran's association.

I believe it is apropos at this point to introduce into this biographical sketch of the Texas Brigade a few words concerning their most famous commander. John Bell Hood was a Kentuckian by birth and a Texan by choice. He was graduated from West Point in the Class of 1853 ranking 44th in a class of 52. After serving with the infantry a few months, Hood was assigned to the famous Second United States Cavalry and was posted to Texas with that elite regiment in 1855. While in the Lone Star State he achieved some fame as an Indian fighter and his aggressive leadership was much pronounced during this early period of his career. Hood, as so many Southern born officers did, resigned his commission in the Old Army and was appointed a 1st Lieutenant of cavalry in the Confederate Armed Forces.

This Kentuckian turned Texan had the greatest advancement in rank of any officer on either side. He rose from 1st Lieutenant to full

General in a little over three years time. Hood was badly wounded at Gettysburg, his left arm being mangled by a shell fragment, and before his wound has sufficiently healed and while his arm was still in a sling, he joined his division for the battle of Chickamauga. Here, on the second day of battle he was hit by a Minieball a few inches below his hip, shattering his right leg, which was amputated at a field hospital close to the front lines. After a few months of recuperation in Richmond, Major-General Hood was promoted to Lieutenant-General and re-assigned to the Army of Tennessee. Because of his infirmities, he rode strapped in his saddle for the rest of the war using his one good arm to hold the reins. His spare mount carried a cork leg that the men of the Texas Brigade had purchased for him from England. Hood, however, preferred a crutch to the artificial limb, but carried the cork leg with him the rest of the war. Most Civil War scholars agree that John Bell Hood was one of the best battlefield leaders in the War. As a brigade and division commander he had few equals, but, as events proved, he was unsuited for corps and army command.

Following the War, Hood, the Episcopalian, married an Irish Catholic girl, Anna Maria Hennen. She was from a well-known New Orleans family, her father was a prominent lawyer in New Orleans and her grandfather had been a Justice of the Supreme Court of Louisiana. The Hoods bought a home and settled down in New Orleans, where the General engaged in the cotton brokerage and the insurance business. Eleven children were born to John Bell and Anna Hood in ten years, including three sets of twins. This, of course, is quite remarkable considering the physical handicaps of the General, but it only goes to prove that Hood was just as aggressive in the boudoir as he was on the battlefield.

Unfortunately, the Hood story has an unhappy ending. His wife, his eldest daughter and the General all died from yellow fever within a few weeks time in 1879, leaving ten orphaned children. His mother-in-law Hennen, in whose custody the children had been left, died within a few months of General Hood, and the custody of the children passed to her brother who in turn gave the ten children up for adoption. Six were placed with Southern families and four with Northern families; this gesture, he hoped, would help to bind the wounded country together.

After Hood was promoted to major-general and given command of a division in the summer of 1862, an assortment of colonels and generals took over command of the Brigade — all of them capable. Colonel William T. Wofford of the 18th Georgia Infantry, commanded the Texas Brigade at bloody Antietam. Brigadier General Jerome Bonaparte Robertson (a physician), who was destined to command the Brigade longer than any other officer, led it to glory at Gettysburg and Chickamauga. (Incidentally, eight of the thirty-two original company commanders of the three Texas Regiments in the Brigade were physicians.) General John Gregg, a lawyer by profession, succeeded Robertson in command and was killed leading the charge at Darbytown Road (October 7, 1864). Gregg would be the only commander of the Brigade to be killed in battle and was the last general officer to command the Texans in Lee's Army. Upon Gregg's death, Colonel C. M. Winkler, then Colonel Frederick S. Bass and finally Colonel Robert H. Powell succeeded each predecessor in command. Powell was in command when Hood's Texas Brigade surrendered its torn battle flags and well-used Enfields at Appomattox Court House in April, 1865.

The war record of this famous fighting unit was a gallant and a glorious one. It was a record written in blood, battlesmoke and bandages from the swamps of the Chickahominy to the rocks of Devil's Den and to the scrub oaks of The Wilderness. Hood's Texas Brigade fought in all of the major battles engaged in by the Army of Northern Virginia except Chancellorsville, and it more than made up for missing this battle by fighting with the Army of Tennessee at Chickamauga and Knoxville and with Longstreet at Suffolk. Lauded by Lee and feared by the Federals, the stubborn Texans often acted as the van in the advance and as the rear guard in retreat, battle positions reserved only for dependable and tenacious fighters.

The brigade was present at 38 engagements that spanned a time period from Eltham's Landing, May 7, 1862, to Appomattox Court House, April 9, 1865, and ranged in intensity from the two casualties at Rice's Depot (April 6, 1865) to the 638 casualties at 2nd Manassas (August 29-30, 1862). Not included in this 38 figure was the roasting ears fight on August 23, 1862, and the great snowball fight that took place January 9, 1863. In the former scrap the Texans and Yanks (of Sigel's Command) bombarded each other with ears of corn in the midst of a 100 acre cornfield in a fight for food. Not one shot was fired and the Texans finally chased the New Yorkers out of the maize patch. In the second hassle the Texas Brigade started a snow-ball fight that eventually involved almost 15,000 "Rebel Yelling" Confederates and had the Federals across the Rappahannock saddling up awaiting what appeared to be a Confederate attack on their position. Mounted officers urged their men on, the bands played and the bugles blew and the mass of snowballs thrown almost obliterated the January sun. Some soldiers cheated and put rocks in the center of their snowballs, an arrangement which caused numerous contusions and fractures. Such actions motivated Lee to issue a General Order prohibiting snowballing in the future in the Army of North Virginia.

The Brigade participated in six of the greatest battles of the War and in these six battles sustained total casualties (killed, wounded and missing) of 3,470. A breakdown of this casualty figure shows the loss at Gaines' Mill (June 27, 1862) to be 623; 2nd Manassas (Aug. 29-30, 1862) 638; Antietam (Sept. 17, 1862) 519; Gettysburg (July 1-3, 1863) 597; Chickamauga (Sept. 19-20, 1863) 570; and the Wilderness (May 6, 1864) 523. I have termed the period from June 27 to September 17, 1862, as the "83 Bloody Days." In this short span of time (less than three months) during the summer of 1862, the Brigade fought in three major battles (Gaines' Mill, 2nd Manassas and Antietam) and suffered an estimated 1,780 casualties. Strength-wise the Brigade was never to recover fully from this early bloodletting.

At the Battle of Antietam or Sharpsburg (the costliest one day of battle in modern warfare) the 1st Texas Infantry Regiment of the Brigade suffered the greatest casualty rate of any regiment, North or South, for a single day's action during the war. According to Livermore, 82.3% of its men on September 17, 1862 were either killed, wounded or missing — most of the casualties being sustained within a one hour period in Miller's cornfield. At this same engagement, the Texas Brigade, as a whole, suffered 64.1% casualties, which was the third highest casualty rate for any brigade, North or South, for a single day's action during the war.

The Texas Brigade had many fine hours during the War — the charge of the Fourth Texas up Turkey Hill at Gaines' Mill, the stand of the First Texas in Miller's Cornfield at Antietam, and the battle around the Viniard House at Chickamauga, to name a few. The Brigades' finest hour, however, was at the battle of The Wilderness on May 6, 1864.

On the first day of battle (May 5) Lee had attacked Grant's ponderous army in flank as it slowly moved south through "The Wilderness" toward Richmond. After heavy fighting the first day with no apparent advantage to either side, Grant renewed the battle at sunrise on May 6 when Hancock's Corps struck Lee's Right Wing under A. P. Hill. Hancock's savage attack routed the divisions of Heth and Wilcox, and Lee in dismay watched his Right Wing melt away. The situation was desperate for the Army of Northern Virginia. Half of

A. P. Hill's Corps was shattered and in retreat and Longstreet's relief corps was still several miles from the battlefield. Lee, understandably, was noticeably shaken by the large numbers of Confederate soldiers fleeing the field; he had not witnessed such a scene before.

Longstreet's Corps, marching the last mile at the double-quick encouraged by the sound of the guns, arrived on the battlefield at the critical moment. With the Texas Brigade and Barksdale's Mississippians leading the way, Old Pete's veterans threading their way though Hill's demoralized men deployed to dispute Hancock's advance. The Texas Brigade, after passing an anxious Robert E. Lee and staff, left the Orange Plank Road and formed their battle line in a large clearing north of the road near the Widow Tapp's House. As in previous battles the Third Arkansas was positioned on the left flank and the First, Fourth and Fifth Texas were posted successively to the right of the Arkansans.

Gregg upon receiving orders from Longstreet "to advance his troops" rode to the center of his command and facing the men shouted, "Attention, Texas Brigade! The eyes . . . of General Lee . . . are upon you! Forward . . . March." As the 800 veterans who had fought many campaigns under Lee advanced toward Hancock's Corps, not 300 yards away, there occurred one of the most dramatic moments in American military history. General Lee with some trepidation and uneasiness watched the scene unfold before him as he sat with his staff near the Widow Tapp's House. Suddenly, he spurred Traveller forward to the rear of the Texas Brigade, removed his grey felt hat and lifting himself in the stirrups was heard by those veterans nearest to him say, "Texans always move them." The General then rode Traveller through an opening between the 1st and 4th Texas and attempted to lead the Texas Brigade into battle. Those soldiers nearest to General Lee ran out of line and surrounding Traveller grabbed at his reins and saddle trappings to stop him. Words to the effect of, "General Lee to the rear," "We won't go forward until you go back," "Go back, General Lee, Go back," were heard on all sides. Finally, Colonel Charles Venable of Lee's staff, aided by General Gregg, "forcibly" persuaded the General to leave the field and return to a place of safety. It is doubtful if Lee would have survived the charge that followed.

After General Lee was conducted to the rear, the Texas Brigade advanced rapidly to the front, so quickly in fact they left the supporting brigades of Benning and Law far behind. Here at The Wilderness, in the autumn of the Confederacy, Hood's Texas Brigade reached the zenith of its remarkable wartime record. The Brigade was reduced now to a hard core of some 800 battle-hardened and dedicated combat veterans — the weak, the maligners and the sick had been dropped from the rolls, under a galling cross-fire that swept across the clearing of Widow Tapp's Farm they moved rapidly into the heavily forested area to their front. Here they engaged Hancock's men in hand-to-hand fighting.

In this determined attack under the eyes of General Lee, the Texans arrested the advance of Hancocks Corps and drove it back to its entrenchments of the night before. Breaking this defense line, the Brigade drove the Federals back to a second line of breastworks, thus advancing unsupported almost 500 yards against greatly superior numbers. But their ranks were shattered! Finally intense flank fire from Federal troops behind breastworks south of the Orange Plank Road and Federal artillery using double-shotted canister firing up the road stopped the advance. Division commander, General Charles Field, fearing that Gregg's small brigade would be cut off and annihilated, ordered it back to reform and replenish its ammunition. The supporting brigades of Benning and Law then came up and continued to press the attack.

The sacrificial assault of the Texas Brigade on the morning of May 6, 1864, was best summed up by General Evander Law, commander of the Alabama Brigade, which supported the Texans during the attack. Law wrote,

> The Federals . . . were advancing through the pines with apparently resistless force, when Gregg's 800 Texans [and Arkansans] dashed directly upon them. There was a terrible crash, mingled with wild yelling [the Rebel Yell] which settled down into a steady roar of musketry. In less than ten minutes one-half of that devoted 800 was lying on the field dead or wounded; but they had delivered a staggering blow and had broken the force of the Federal advance.

No wonder Lee had once said "that he relied on his Texans in all the tight places." Although it decimated the Brigade, the Texans never let their commander down.

It has been estimated that some 4,500 men fought under the shredded battle flags of the three Texas Regiments of the Brigade. At Appomattox, after almost four years of arduous service, but 476 or a little over ten percent of these soldiers were left to surrender. Bullets and disease had killed hundreds, and hundreds more had been invalided home from crippling wounds and prolonged sieges of sickness — few had deserted! The 3rd Arkansas sustained like casualties.

Besides the hell of shot and shell that rained on the Brigade, its members were exposed to the rigors of long marches and inclement and intense weather during their numerous campaigns. The East Tennessee Campaign conducted during the winter of 1863-64 was a particularly trying one. The temperature was often freezing with snow on the ground, and while one fourth of the men were actually without shoes, all had to be content with worn out footwear, tattered uniforms, threadbare blankets and rancid or no rations. Wherever they marched, the jagged ice and frozen roads cut their feet and gave the snow a crimson hue. Opposite conditions prevailed during the march from Texas to New Orleans in the summer of 1861, the companies of the 4th and 5th Texas had to wade through the swamps and mud of lower Louisiana during the rainy season and combat alligators, snakes and swarms of mosquitoes in the process. The wonder of it all is how even 476 men were still able to answer the roll call at Appomattox.

While the members of Hood's Brigade amassed an enviable record on the battlefield they also gained the reputation of being the best foragers in the Army of Northern Virginia. Foraging, which abounds in wartime, is a time-honored practice for armies in the field. Foraging is the polite military term which embraces such disreputable civilian practices as rustling, shoplifting, smuggling and stealing; filching and fleecing; and pillaging, plundering, poaching and "pinching" — as our English cousins call it. Foraging is often spoken of as "moonlight requisitioning," but it was carried out by the Texans during daylight hours as well.

The deftness of Hood's Texans in raiding barnyards and chicken coops, in particular, was recognized by the Confederate high command. It was either General Pete Longstreet or General Dick Anderson who, when asked by a *London Times* reporter what kind of fighters the Texans in Hood's Texas Brigade were, replied, "the Texas boys are great fighters, none better. But they are purely hell on chickens and shoats." Robert E. Lee, one evening after Fredericksburg, remarked in Hood's presence that he was alarmed at the depradations committed on the local farmers by the Army of Northern Virginia. Hood, no doubt with tongue in cheek, immediately protested the innocence of his men to such delinquencies. Lee with a twinkle in his eye turned toward Hood, remarking, "Ah, General Hood, when you Texans come about the chickens have to roost high." Lt. Col. J. A. L. Fremantle, like Col. Wolsely, an observer from the British Army, attached himself to Lee's Army during the Gettysburg Campaign and became acquainted with Hood and his Texans during this time. "Hood's troops," Fremantle wrote, "were accused of being a wild set and difficult to manage; and it is the great object of the chiefs to check their innate plundering propensitied by every means in their power."

Many stories abound of the ingenious attempts made by the Texans to replace their ragged raiments and their crushed chapeaus and to augment their rancid rations at the expense of the local civilians North and South. In most instances the boys from the Lone Star State were eminently successful in their endeavors and thus deserved the reputation that they enjoyed in this area of military pursuit. If something moved or looked like it was going to move, or looked like it was even alive, it was fair game for the Texans. Surely the anonymous lyricist who composed the following Civil War rhyme had Hood's Texans in mind when he wrote,

> Hark! I hear a rooster squall;
> The vandal takes it hen and all,
> And makes the boys and women bawl,
> Here's your mule, O here's your mule.

This sticky-fingered inclination of the Texans showed its hand early in the war, as a matter of fact even before the companies left Texas and while they were still in "boot camp" at Camp Van Dorn near Harrisburg, a small hamlet six miles east of Houston on Buffalo Bayou. The Lone Star Guards from Waco had been at Camp Van Dorn only a few days when private Dick Jones strode through the tented area with a huge turkey gobbler thrown over his shoulder. The commander of the Waco Company, Captain Ed Ryan, who had issued a "no foraging" order was attracted to the scene by the shouts of the men and the frantic gobbles of Old Tom. Ryan intercepted Jones and demanded an explanation. With a straight face Jones protested "that the turkey tried to bite him and he did not intend to be imposed upon." A few days later Ed Tilly and Andy Wollard of the Waco Company, nosing around farms in the vicinity of Camp, killed a fat shoat which indiscreetly was rubbing its back against an outside fence. The boys, in this case, were diplomatic enough to present Captain Ryan with a nice piece of roast pork, so few questions were asked.

The Post Exchange and Commissary facilities of the modern military service were provided in the Civil War by the infamous Sutler's system and by itinerant peddlers and merchants from nearby towns. While there were exceptions to the rule, generally the Sutlers and peddlers were unscrupulous get-rich-quick merchants. They overpriced their wares, fostered drunkenness, extended excessive credit and then collected by liens against the soldier's pay. The Texans were particularly hard on operators of this type and in at least two instances on record "foraged" them out of business. However, in fairness to the record, at least one of the peddlers took his revenge on the Lone Star punsters.

While the Brigade was camped near the Mechanicsville Pike outside of Richmond after the battle of Seven Pines, one of the peddlers from the Confederate Capital selling sausage slipped a fast one over on one group of Texans. The messing group that Bill Fletcher belonged to in the Fifth Texas had purchased a good deal of sausage meat from a particular merchant from town. One morning, a day or two after the purchase and after the merchant had pulled up stakes and vanished, various members of the mess found cat claws, teeth, fur and other parts of the feline anatomy ground up and embedded in the sausage. Fletcher reported that "some of the boys tried to vomit, but the cat kept on its downward course." Substituting felines for porkers in the sausage was a feather in the cap of the merchant who was smart enough to move on before he was mobbed by his bilious Texas customers.

Besides being great combat troops and successful foragers, Hood's Texans had a fine sense of humor, a trait which helped to make their hard life of soldiering bearable. The following incident I think well illustrates this quality. On June 27, 1863, on their way to the battle of Gettysburg the Texans passed through Chambersburg, Pennsylvania. The fair sex of the town lined the streets, hanging over the front yard fences, gabbing back and forth and hurling taunts and jibes at the ragged Rebel Army as it tramped through. Many of the women had miniature United States flags pinned to their dresses and others were waving small flags. One particularly well-proportioned female standing at the front door of her home draped a large American flag across her bulging bosom. Thus, she stood at attention with contempt written on her face as Lee's army passed by. As the Texans tramped by, one of them, noticing the magnificent matron, said in a solemn voice, raised above the noise of the shuffling feet, "Take care, madam, for Hood's boys are great at storming breastworks, particularly when the Yankee colors are on them." Needless to say the buxom beauty beat a bashful retreat.

The members of Hood's Brigade, while not the rowdiest soldiers in the Army of Northern Virginia, did their share of hell raising on the march and in bivouac. On the way to Gettysburg, after crossing the Potomac from Virginia to Maryland one of the few wholesale drinking orgies, engaged in by those Texans associated with Lee, took place. It seems that a large store of Federal whiskey had been confiscated by the Confederate Army in the vicinity of Hagerstown, Maryland, and orders were issued to distribute the social liquid among the

Southern soldiers. Hood, not to be left out of any liquid ration, requested and received more than a few barrels of the demon rum for his division. He ordered that a whiskey ration of one gill (1/4 pt.) per man be distributed to the various brigades. The men who did not drink passed their ration on to a buddy who was not above imbibing now and then, and there the trouble started. The combination of a long march, scanty rations, an empty stomach, the excitement of a campaign in Yankeedom and a few gills of whiskey was just plain disastrous.

John Stevens reported,
> that inside half an hour there were more drunk men in Williamsport, Maryland than I think I ever saw in my life . . . they were drunk all over, through and through, up and down, side, edge and fore and aft. It kept the sober boys busy to keep the drunk ones from killing each other. Some soon fell by the wayside helpless and were dumped into wagons and ambulances and hauled the balance of the day. Some others were not seen for fifteen hours afterwards and when they caught up with their commands they were quite sober but their eyes looked like "two burnt holes in a blanket."

Concerning the same incident, Brigade Historian J. B. Polley remembered that the quantity of whiskey available "was amply sufficient to put fully half the brigade not only in a boisterously good humor, but such physical condition that the breadth of the road over which they marched that evening was more of an obstacle to rapid progress than its length."

Finally the Brigade was reformed in some semblance of order and marched across the narrow neck of Maryland to the vicinity of Greencastle, Pennsylvania, to cook supper and bivouac for the night. The men of Hood's Division on June 26, 1863, performed a feat never performed by any other Confederate troops during the war. They ate breakfast in Virginia, lunch in the state of Maryland, supper in Pennsylvania, and slept that night in the state of intoxication. Thus encompassing four states within a 24 hour period. Even JEB Stuart's cavalry could not equal this feat.

By the winter of 1864-65, many of the Confederate brigades, due to battle losses and sickness, were much depleted. In preparation for the spring campaign of 1865 Jefferson Davis ordered a consolidation of the smallest brigades. Hood's Texas Brigade, of course, fell in this category. The Texans, proud of their excellent combat record and wishing to maintain their great esprit-de-corps were dead set against involving their Brigade in such a program. Major "Howdy" Martin, colorful and eloquent member of the Fourth Texas Infantry, was selected by his peers to present the Brigade's position to President Davis. Martin, who received his nickname by his informal salute and homely salutation, obtained an audience with the Confederate leader through the offices of the Texan, Postmaster General John H. Reagan. When the flamboyant Martin, with hands waving in the air and his long hair swirling about his face and neck made his "no merger" plea to the Confederate President, General Lee was there. The General, upon hearing the Texan's sincere words, remarked to Davis, "Mr. President, before you pass upon this request, I want to say that I never ordered that Brigade to hold a place that they did not hold it." General Lee's testimonial and Major Martin's resolute and colorful presentation were more than enough to convince the President that to merge the Texas Brigade with another brigade would be a mistake. Turning to the Major, dressed in his ragged, battle-scarred "uniform," Davis said, "Major Martin, as long as there is a man to carry that battle flag, you shall remain a separate brigade."

Hood's Texas Brigade, loyal to the Southern cause, remained defiant to the end. During the six day retreat from Richmond to Appomattox, the Texans served as the rear guard for the Army of Northern Virginia. After marching through an area marked by chaos, clutter and confusion they took up a position about a mile from Appomattox Court House and built crude breastworks. Here they determined to make their final stand at the rear of Lee's Army. The men were ragged, starved and exhausted. They had not eaten for three days except for a little bread that they had hastily made on the march and some kernels of corn they had picked from the ground where cavalry horses had been fed. When word was received that Lee had surrendered, they refused to believe the news. Finally convinced of the fact that the end had come, many of the grizzled old veterans openly wept, others in anger smashed their Enfields against trees breaking the stocks, while others tried to bend the barrels of their guns in tree forks. On the morning of April 10, 1865, the four regiments of the Brigade formed on the color line to hear their officers read Lee's Farewell Address and explain the surrender terms. The end had come at last.

After Appomattox the veterans of Hood's Brigade straggled back to Texas, some individually, others in small groups and still others in large parties. They walked, they went by boat and they rode the rails back to the Lone Star State, each eager to see his family and again embrace his interrupted civilian pursuit. However, the comradeship that had been forged on the anvil of battle and bivouac was not long in re-asserting itself.

In 1872, some 66 members of the famed Brigade met at the Old Hutchins House in Houston to organize Hood's Texas Brigade Association. This Association was one of the strongest and most active veterans' groups to be formed after the War Between the States. It met continually in regular annual reunions for 62 years (through 1933) with the exception of the years 1898 and 1918, the two war years. Lt. Colonel C. M. Winkler served as the first president of the Association, but General J. B. Robertson filled that office the greatest number of times, eleven. June 27 was the date selected for the annual reunions of the Association as this was the anniversary of the Brigade's great breakthrough at Gaines' Mill, its first big victory of the War!

Communities in Central and East Texas vied with each other to host these annual meetings of the old soldiers. Twenty-nine different Texas towns and cities during the Association's sixty-two years of existence shared in this hosting honor. However, commencing in 1919 and every year thereafter until the last reunion in 1933, Hood's Veterans met in Bryan, Texas, which has termed itself, and rightfully so, the "last home of Hood's Texas Brigade."

It was customary for governors, senators and generals to attend the annual reunions of the Brigade Association and pay homage to those veterans in gray, who, for four long years, had excited the imagination of the entire world with their dash, their devotion and their determination.

Lt. Bolling Eldridge of Company E of the Fifth Texas was the last known survivor of Hood's Texas Brigade, the last mortal link of this great group of fighters to the sunny Southland. Eldridge passed away at his home in Brenham, Texas, on October 29, 1938, at the age of 95. On that October 29, 1938 the last tattoo for Hood's Texas Brigade was sounded. An era in Confederate and Texas History had ended and another brigade of the Army of Northern Virginia was dropped from the master rolls.

> The muffled drums' sad roll has beat
> The soldiers' last tattoo:
> No more on life's parade shall meet
> That brave and fallen few.
> On fame's eternal camping ground
> Their silent tents are spread
> And glory guards with solemn sound
> The bivouac of the dead.

Whether acting in the capacity of scouts, skirmishers, sharp-shooters or line of battle fighters, the soldiers of Hood's Texas Brigade had few, if any, equals in the annals of American fighting men from the Battle of Bunker Hill to the Battle of the Bulge. This unit was a credit to its American Heritage, a credit to the famous Army in which it fought and a credit to the State that it represented.

"Not for fame or reward, not for place or rank, not lured by ambition or goaded by necessity. But in simple obedience to duty as they understood it, these men suffered all, sacrificed all, endured all . . . and died." May Americans, and especially Texans, never forget the heroic deeds of Hood's Texas Brigade, the bravest of the brave and among the finest infantry in United States history.

CAMELS, JEFF DAVIS AND TEXAS
THE U.S. ARMY'S CAMEL CORPS

— COMPANY OF MILITARY HISTORIANS

UNCLE SAM'S CAMEL CORPS
A CIVILIAN, AN ARMY SERGEANT, A MULE SKINNER, AND A CAMEL DRIVER PREPARING FOR THE CAMEL EXPEDITION FROM TEXAS TO CALIFORNIA, 1857.

CAMELS, JEFF DAVIS AND TEXAS

Before taking up the story of the U.S. Army's experiment with camels in the late 1850's, an experiment which I believe to be one of the most interesting and unusual in our nation's military history, I believe that we should discuss the physical attributes and the personality of the hero of my presentation, the camel.

There are basically two types of camels, the *Arabian* and the *Bactrian*. The Arabian is found primarily in North Africa, Asia Minor, and Arabia. It has one large hump on the back and is a rather tall, gangling animal. The Bactrian, on the other hand, is found principally in Eastern Turkey and North Central Asia, and it is primarily a heavyset, shaggy-haired, slow animal. It is sometimes used in harness and has two humps on its back.

Three modifications of these two basic types of camels exist: the dromedary, the Booghdee and the Pehlevan. The dromedary is a lightweight, tall, fast Arabian used as a personnel carrier. The Booghdee is a cross between a Bactrian male and an Arabian female. It is a very large, one-humped camel with great endurance, and is called a "mule camel" by Americans. The Pehlevan is a wrestling camel of Arabian stock. It has short front legs and a powerful neck. Pehlevan camels are best known in Turkey where camel wrestling is considered a major sport.

When traveling, camels can go as long as five days without water, although normally they drink every third day. When grazing and not working they can go without water for weeks if dew is present. The male camel comes into season and not the female. The female produces one (1) young at birth, and the camel does not reach complete maturity until its sixteenth or seventeenth year. The normal life span of the camel is 40 years. Some live to be 50. While this interesting beast of burden can carry over 1,000 pounds for a short distance, the normal load of an Arabian is 400 to 600 pounds, and for the Bactrian 600 to 800 pounds. The camel usually travels two to four miles per hour. It can travel at this rate for six to twelve hours per day, but will actually keep going until it drops dead. One hundred miles per day is not unusual for a good Arabian saddle breed. The normal gait is the pace, but they may trot or even gallop when properly prodded. The camel is the most contemptuous and bored of all animals, and is considered by many experts to have a very low intelligence.

There are several unusual physical features and/or characteristics of the camel that make him adaptable to wasteland and desert travel. Extra heavy eyebrows and eyelids protect his eyes from the sun and sand. He has an acute sense of sight and smell and can smell water as far as a mile away. Large calluses on the leg joints (knees) and the chest protect these parts from abrasion while kneeling or lying down. Small hoofs are situated at the end of the two toes on each foot, and the padded soles of the feet afford good traction on both sand and rock. The camel has a particularly thick tongue, tough lips and surprisingly strong jaws in order to eat the thick and thorny desert and wasteland plants. They have three stomachs which consist of numerous compartments or sections that store and slowly release water. Camels possess a hump or humps which contain fat storage for ready energy. Other than for transportation, the camel is a source of weavable hair, palatable milk and flesh and utilizable hide and bones. Thus the camel is to the nomad of the desert what the bison was to the Indian, their chief means of subsistence and a source for food, clothing and shelter.

Camels also have a few undesirable traits which one must be aware of. They have a vicious bite that can break an arm with one snap. They constantly chew on a cud composed of their forage material and they can spit this slimy substance ten to twelve feet with great accuracy. And too, at times, they possess, a strong and pungent odor.

So much for the camel. Now let us take a look at the man who was most responsible for its introduction into the United States, Jefferson Davis. Davis is perhaps best known to you as the President of the Confederate States of America. Unfortunately for Davis, I think, the American public remembers him best in this ill-fated role. However, previous to his denunciation of the Union in early 1861 he was one of America's foremost senators, an outstanding secretary of war, and a better than average professional soldier.

Davis was born in Christian County, Kentucky, not far from the birthplace of Abraham Lincoln, on June 3, 1808. He graduated from the United States Military Academy at West Point in 1828 and served in the United States Army on the western frontier until 1835. In that year he married Zachary Taylor's daughter, resigned his commission, and settle in Mississippi as a cotton planter. Davis was elected a member of Congress in 1845, but resigned his seat in 1846 to fight when the United States declared war against Mexico. Davis organized the first Mississippi Volunteer Infantry Regiment, better known as "The Mississippi Rifles." This regiment was composed of wealthy young Mississippi planters like himself and was assigned to General Zachary Taylor's army in Northern Mexico. The Mississippi Rifles Regiment was not only one of the best fighting units in the war, but it was also one of the most colorful and best equipped. The young planters wore white duck trousers, fireman red flannel shirts, and wide-brimmed Panama hats. Each member of the regiment had his own personal body servant, carried the new "Mississippi Rifle," possessed the most expensive accoutrements and smoked Havana cigars. In other words, they were an elite regiment, proud of their state and proud of their commander.

The Mississippi Rifles fought in two major engagements during the Mexican War, Monterrey and Buena Vista, and it was in the later battle that they earned their fame as a fighting regiment. General Taylor ordered the "Rifles" to support Captain Braxton Bragg's Artillery Battery that was trying to stem the advance of an attack against Taylor's rear by Mexican lancers. The Mississippi Rifles successfully defended the position but suffered many casualties — their leader being one of them. The wounded Davis returned to his Mississippi plantation to recuperate amid the accolades of the nation as "the Hero of Buena Vista," a title later more properly accorded to General Taylor.

In 1847 the Governor of Mississippi appointed Davis to fill an unexpired seat in the United States Senate, and he was officially elected to fill this same seat at the next senatorial election. While a member of the Senate, Davis served as chairman of the Committee on Military Affairs.

In 1852 when a fellow Democrat, Franklin Pierce of Hillsboro, New Hampshire, was elected President, Davis was appointed to his cabinet as the Secretary of War. Jefferson Davis proved to be one of the most able and most progressive Secretaries of War that the United States has ever had, and rates with John C. Calhoun and Elihu Root, I believe, as the best men to-date to have filled that position. During Davis' term as Secretary of War, the United States Military Academy at West Point was enlarged and the curriculum improved. He increased the size of the Army better to protect the frontier from Indian depredations, he sought (but unfortunatly without success) to abolish the Army Seniority Rule which he regarded as a serious handicap, he planned and directed the surveys for the railroad routes to the Pacific and last but not least he introduced the camel into the United States Army. It is, of course, with this last event that we are primarily concerned.

After serving as the Secretary of War from 1853 to 1857, Davis was again elected to the Senate from Mississippi. He served in this August body until January 21, 1861, when he resigned to return to his native state where he had been appointed a major-general and commander of the State Militia — Mississippi had left the Union on

January 9, 1861. On February 10, Davis was elected President of the newly formed Confederate States of America and took the oath of office at Montgomery, Alabama, on February 18. You know the rest of his story from there on.

After this capsule history of the camel and Davis, our two main characters, the stage is now set to discuss this unusual experiment in United States Military History. Two army officers, Majors George H. Crossman and Henry C. Wayne were the first major proponents for the importation of camels. Major Crossman was probably the first person to discuss this idea seriously and as early as 1836 he tried to interest the Washington authorities in importing camels for use in the Second Seminole War (1835-42). Major Wayne, who had a distinguished Mexican War record as an artillerist, had made a detailed study of the camel and was convinced that this animal was the only answer to our military logistics problem in the Southwest. In 1848 Wayne proposed to the War Department that they buy camels from the Near East for service on our Western Frontier. While no action was taken on Wayne's suggestion at the time, he did succeed in interesting Jefferson Davis, then a Senator from Mississippi, in the feasibility of his plan.

Davis was extremely interested in military affairs, and he visualized the camel as the answer to the problem of supplying our military outposts in Texas and in the Arizona Territory. It was of great concern to Davis that it took 120 days of tedious overland travel to go from West Texas to our defenseless Pacific Coast. Knowing the capability of the camel to operate in an arid region (such as the trek from Texas to Southern California embraced), he was even more convinced that the United States government should import a large number of these animals for experimental purposes. Fortunately, Jeff Davis, unlike the other advocates of a camel corps, was in a position to take some direct action on the matter. In 1851, as Chairman of the Senate Military Affairs Committee, Davis made the first attempt to obtain government backing for the camel project. In March of that year he recommended that $30,000 be appropriated for the purchase of camels and the hiring of a suitable number of Arab drivers and handlers. However, Davis's plan lacked the necessary senatorial support and was disapproved by a 24 to 19 vote.

The Mississippi Senator was not discouraged by this initial setback and was more determined than ever to see the project through. In concert with Major Wayne he made an extensive study of the various breeds of camels and their uses and employment throughout the world. One year later in 1852, armed with this additional information on the camel, he succeeded in convincing his colleagues in the Senate that it was a worthwhile project; unfortunately, the House of Representatives, which had not been exposed to Davis' convincing arguments on the subject, ridiculed the Senate's action and voted the scheme down.

By 1853 Davis was the Secretary of War in Franklin Pierce's Cabinet and now was in an even better position to push his pet project. He convinced President Pierce of the practicability of importing camels for the purpose of solving the military logistics problems in the Southwest, and together they went to work on Congress. Pierce as Commander of the New England Brigade in Scott's Army during the Mexican War, had been allotted 1,000 wild mules to move his brigade from Vera Cruz to Puebla and was thoroughly disgusted with mules, so the camel experiment appealed to him. Although Davis mentioned the Camel Project in his annual reports to Congress in both 1853 and 1854, it fell on deaf ears. However, Senator James Shields of Illinois, incidentally the only man to serve as a Senator from three states, championed the camel cause in the Senate and amended the Annual Army Appropriation Bill of 1855 by attaching an appropriation of $30,000 "to be expended under the direction of the War Department in the purchase and importation of camels and dromedaries to be employed for military purposes." The amended bill passed both the Senate and the House of Representatives on March 3, 1855. Thus, after eight years of labor, Jeff Davis saw his idea for an experimental camel corps materialize and he lost no time in implementing the Congressional Act which authorized the purchase.

Assistance to help sell his idea to the public came to Davis from an unexpected quarter in the person of George P. Marsh, a well-known writer and world traveler. Marsh was so convinced that the camel was the answer to our military transportation problem in the Southwest that he wrote a small book in 1856 extolling the advantages of the camel. This book was entitled, *The Camel, His Organization, Habits, and Uses Considered With Reference to His Introduction into the United States*, and was widely circulated throughout the country, thus helping to prepare the American public for the experiment.

The Secretary of War personally selected the three men who were to procure and transport the camels back to the United States. Major Wayne, the army officer who had worked with Davis in 1851 and 1852 in researching on the breeds and uses of the camel and who had first interested Davis in the experiment back in 1848, was chosen to head the expedition. To assist Wayne, Davis selected Navy

Lieutenant David Dixon Porter because of his "professional ability and energy." It is interesting to note that Porter was forty two (42) years old and had been a naval lieutenant for twenty (20) years. Davis would have cause to remember this name for during the Civil War Porter rose to the rank of admiral in the Union Navy and combining his talents with those of General U. S. Grant severed the Confederacy in 1863. Porter came from a naval family; his father had fought in the un-declared naval war against France in 1798-99, the war with the Barbary Pirates of Tripoli in 1804-05, and the War of 1812. The senior Porter resigned from the United States Navy in 1826, after which he commanded the Mexican Navy for three years, then served as the U.S. Minister to Turkey and finally as the U.S. Consul General at Algiers. Lieutenant Porter was as impetuous and fiery as his father but he showed a marked capacity for infinite detail and care on the camel assignment.

The third man Davis chose for the camel procurement and transportation detail was Gwinn A. Heap, a first cousin of Lieutenant Porter. Heap had been on several exploring parties in the Southwest and knew well the type of terrain the camel would have to become accustomed to in the United States. Heap was also familiar with the customs and the languages of the countries from which the camels were to be procured and in 1855 was residing with his father, the U.S. Consul at Tunis.

Davis gave detailed instructions in writing to his "camel committee" composed of Wayne, Porter and Heap concerning the selection of the camels. The Secretary required them to prepare an extensive report on the camel's needs, diseases it was susceptible to, how to pack the camel, etc. This report is now in the National Archives and is a testimony to the intelligence and the diligence of his three emissaries.

Lieutenant Porter was assigned the ship, the *USS Supply*, a 141 foot, 547 ton storeship to command for the purpose of transporting the camels from the Mediterranean to Texas, where the climate and terrain were thought to be the most favorable for commencing the experiment. The *USS Supply* was at the New York Navy Yard, and Porter went to work immediately to modify the ship as a camel carrier. He sailed from New York on June 3, 1855, with his first port of call being La Spezia, Italy. In the meantime, Major Wayne had left for London and Paris to consult with zoological and military experts in those cities as to the habits, the military uses, and the best places in the Middle East and North Africa to procure camels. Wayne and Porter joined forces in Italy in late July and eager to get on with their project, sailed for Tunis where they were to meet Gwinn Heap, the third member of their committee.

Wayne and Porter arrived at Tunis on August 4, 1855, and, unfortunately, were hoodwinked into purchasing a sad-looking bag of bones before they met their experienced third partner, Heap. The Bey of Tunis, when he learned that the American camel buyers had landed, presented them with 2 fine stallion camels, one full grown and the other young. Using these three camels to test the facilities that Lieutenant Porter had constructed on his ship and to experiment with the management of the ungainly beasts at sea, the Americans left Tunis on August 9 for Constantinople. Word traveled fast through the Mediterranean area that easy American money was to be had and as Major Wayne recorded in his official report, ". . . every sore-backed and superannuated camel in Asia Minor was doctored up and hurried to the coast to be generously offered to the United States at a grievous sacrifice of ten times its value."

On route to Constantinople, the camel cruiser touched at Malta, Smyrna and Solonica and finally arrived at its destination after a voyage of almost 90 days. Attempts were made at the intermediate stops to obtain camels, but British agents had bought up or rented nearly 8,000 camels in this area for use in the Crimean War and the only ones available were either too high in price or worthless. The three camels on board did not seem to have suffered from the voyage, either from the long confinement on shipboard or the rolling and pitching of the *USS Supply* in the rough weather which was encountered. However, the original bag of bones that was purchased in Tunis and one of the Bey's gift camels had developed the "itch," a common camel disease, and both were sold to a butcher in Constantinople.

In early January 1856 the *USS Supply* headed for Smyrna where Heap, the only "camel expert" of the trio, had gone from Tunis the previous month in an attempt to procure enough camels to fill the carefully prepared camel stalls on board ship. At Smyrna they took on 2 male Bactrians, an immense Booghdee female name "Tulu," which weighed over 2,000 pounds and stood 7 feet 4 inches high, 4 male Pehlevans and 15 female Arabians. One of the Arabians, after a short time on board, produced a male foal which was soon trained by the sailors to wrestle. To handle this herd, Wayne hired three Arabs and two Turks as grooms and drivers to accompany the animals. These contract handlers turned out to be practically worthless as Porter's sailors had to attend to most of the camels' needs during the voyage home besides taking care of the seasick camel handlers.

Lieutenant Porter had done a remarkable job in preparing his ship for the cargo of camels and in caring for the animals once they were aboard. Thirty-three separate padded stalls were provided, these were whitewashed and scrubbed daily, clean hay was put in the stalls regularly, and the camels were curried and rubbed down until they glistened. Porter was convinced that the dreaded camel disease, the itch, was caused by uncleanliness of the beasts and their stalls. Because of Porter's precautions not one case of the disease was reported during the voyage home. Porter designed a special harness with which to tie the camels down during rough weather so that they would not get bruised and he also designed a specially built "camel car" to assist in loading the animals on the ship. The one thing that Porter had not counted on was taking on board a camel as large as "Tulu" — to accommodate her large hump a hole had to be cut through the deck over her stall. This made walking on the deck on a moonless night a sporting proposition.

On St. Valentines's Day, February 14, 1856, the Americans with thirty (30) camels on board left Smyrna and started the long voyage home to Texas. It was a very rough crossing, so rough that the vessel could not stop at the Canary Islands as planned to look at the camel herd there. After putting into Kingston, Jamaica, for water (where some 4,000 people visited the ship to see the camels) they arrived off of Indianola, Texas, a port since destroyed by hurricanes and tidal waves, on May 14, 1856, after an eighty-seven day voyage. It had been a most profitable trip — the cost of the camels and contingent expenses did not exceed $8,000. The voyage also definitely proved that the camel had another unique characteristic — it did not get seasick, something that could not be said for the native camel drivers.

Porter proved during the trip that he was not only a first-class naval officer, but also a skilled veterinarian. His skillful breeding of four camels at the proper time on shipboard certainly ranks him as the only officer in the United States Navy to have managed a floating camel stud farm. Porter also acted as midwife at the six births which occurred during the rough winter passage. Four of these young camels died soon after birth and one adult camel died during the voyage; thus the United States Government was one camel to the good when births were balanced against deaths.

The thirty-one (31) camels were actually landed on Powder Point off of Indianola, Texas, which was some 120 miles southwest of Galveston. Although the camels had been well cared for and well fed during their stay aboard the *USS Supply* they were exceedingly glad to see *Terra Firma* after three months of rolling, pitching and yawing. The shipboard problem was compounded by the fact that although they had arrived off of Indianola on April 29, because of bad weather and shallow water, they were not unloaded until May 13. Their pleasure on landing is best described by Porter, who stated,

> ... the camels became excited to an almost uncontrollable degree, rearing, kicking, crying out, breaking halters, tearing up pickets, and by other fantastic tricks demonstrating their enjoyment ... some of the males, becoming pugnacious in their excitement, were with difficulty restrained from attacking each other.

Most of the disbelieving Texans and their horses who were watching the debarkation scattered to the seven winds when the ordinarily placid camels went into their tantrums.

No sooner had the first group of camels been unloaded when Porter and Heap were ordered by the Secretary to return to the Eastern Mediterranean on a second camel procurement mission. After Porter and Heap had departed, the original camel herd under the guidance of Major Wayne proceeded by easy stages to San Antonio. From San Antonio the herd moved about 60 miles northwest to the military post, Camp Verde, near Bandera, Texas. Here, a permanent camel corral or khan was established in August, 1856.

When the camels were passing through the town of Victoria on their journey from Indianola to San Antonio, a Mrs. Mary Shirkey, a recent emigree from Virginia, plucked a sizeable wad of hair from the animals. This hair she proceeded to knit into a pair of socks for the Chief Executive. Wayne forwarded the socks through channels to Davis for Pierce, and we must presume that these camel hair socks (the first to be knitted in the United States) eventually adorned the feet of the "Young Hickory from the Granite Hills."

Major Wayne lost no time in getting the herd and its quarters at Camp Verde in tip-top shape, and by September, mixed camel, mule and horse convoys were being sent to San Antonio for supplies. Even during these relatively short trips to the Mission City and back (120 miles) in the fall months of 1856, the camel proved its superiority over both the horse and the mule. Wayne reported to Davis that six camels carried as much as twelve horses could haul in wagons, and in almost half the time. He stated also that the camels could negotiate, without fatigue, muddy roads which would mire down the horses and wagons and that the camel could travel with ease over mountain paths where wagons couldn't even venture. By the end of 1856 the camels were working out so well that Davis in his annual report to the President and to Congress could state that the camel experiment was succeeding.

How did the Texans regard the invasion of their range land by this peculiar looking newcomer? The camel was viewed with mixed emotions. He was a curiosity piece, there is no doubt, for with his peculiar lurching gait, his awkward appearance, and supercilious and aloof airs, he attracted a crowd wherever he went. On the other hand, just the sight or smell of a "hump backed horse," which the Texans called the camels, drove the horses to a frenzy of bucking and snorting and runaways were the order of the day. This reaction of the horses was serious, for the Texan and his horse were inseparable except when they saw a camel and then usually the horse went one way and the rider another.

Major Wayne, in order to impress the local inhabitants with the weight-carrying ability of the camel, had a driver take one of the larger animals to the Quartermaster Forage Depot at Indianola to get four bales of hay. As usual, when the camels came into town, a large crowd gathered and followed it to the government depot. There, in view of many of the town's inhabitants, the camel was made to kneel and two bales of hay, weighing over 300 pounds apiece, were packed on and then two more bales were tied on the pack saddle, making a total load of over 1200 pounds as much as two horses could carry in a wagon. Under this heavy load the camel rose, back legs first, and lumbered nonchalantly off, much to the astonishment of the onlookers. Feats like this impressed the public with the feasibility of Jeff Davis' experiment.

Porter returned from his second and final camel procurement voyage on February 10, 1857, with forty-one Arabian and Bactrian camels of both sexes. He also brought back eight Greek, Arabian and Turkish camel drivers. The United States government's camel herd was now composed of eighty camels, seventy-five of which had been imported plus 5 births that had occurred since landing. The entire herd was concentrated at Camp Verde waiting for instruction from Washington to begin their formal cross-country test.

In March, 1857, James Buchanan succeeded Franklin Pierce as President of the United States, and John B. Floyd of Virginia, who later was to become an unsuccessful Confederate General, replaced Jefferson Davis as the Secretary of War. Unfortunately for the camel experiment, Floyd did not have the drive or vision of Davis, and too, he was occupied with the so-called Mormon War in Utah. The camels lost another friend also when Major Wayne was ordered to duty in Washington during the change in administrations.

However, by a stroke of good fortune the camel herd passed into capable hands when Secretary Floyd appointed, in the spring of 1857, a former-naval lieutenant, Edward Fitzgerald Beale, to conduct the crosscountry trek from Texas to California, using the camels as pack animals. The trip was to be the acid test of the camel's ability to traverse the arid and rough country of West Texas and New Mexico.

By the spring of 1857 the herd of camels was fast becoming a mecca for distinguished visitors. On March 29 of that year two officers from the Second United States Cavalry, who were soon to become famous on opposite sides during the Civil War, Lieut-Colonel Robert E. Lee and Major George H. Thomas, inspected the camel experimental station at Camp Verde. Colonel Lee liked what he saw and predicted that the camel's "endurance, docility, and sagacity will not fail to attract the attention of the new Secretary of War . . ."

By late June, 1857 all was in readiness to test the camel's adaptability to the American Southwest. A survey trip for a wagon road from Texas to California along the 35th parallel was the project selected for the test. It was decided to take 25 camels on the trek and this number had been moved from Camp Verde to San Antonio where they were to be loaded for their trip. Horses, mules and camels were all three to be used so that the capabilities of each animal under exactly the same conditions could be fairly assessed. A hitch developed at the last minute when the imported camel drivers and attendants refused to make the long trip to California alleging that they had been badly treated by the government for they had not received their pay since the previous January. However, it was believed that the real reason that they refused to go was that they had recently observed some of the Indian's handiwork with the scalping knife. So, at the eleventh hour soldiers and civilian mule drivers had to take on-the-job training from the native drivers on how to pack and care for the camels. The Americans never did learn how to pack the camels properly; it seemed like they could not quite solve the problem of what to do with the hump. This poor back packing would serve as a handicap to the camels during the experiment.

Beale and one of his assistants, M. H. Stacey, kept day by day diaries during the trip, and as the party proceeded westward both of them became more and more impressed with the work of the "ships of the desert." The party left San Antonio at 1 p.m. on June 25, 1857, and on the first day out Beale reported that sixteen miles were made that afternoon and that each camel carried ". . . including pack saddles, nearly six hundred pounds."

On June 28 the caravan had reached Uvalde, Texas, and Beale was particularly impressed with the eating habits of the camel. He states as follows,

> As soon as they arrive in camp they are turned loose to graze, but appear to prefer to browse in the Mesquite Bushes and leaves of a thorny shrub, which grows in this country everywhere, to the finest grass. They are exceedingly docile, easily managed, and I see, so far, no reason to doubt the success of the experiment.

Beale also noted another point in favor of the camel, because of their placidity and dislike of galloping they were virtually stampede-proof.

On July 11 when traveling down the valley of the Pecos River over flinty gravel, Beale enthusiastically remarked,

> The camels . . . have not evinced the slightest distress or soreness: and this is the more remarkable, as mules or horses, in a very short time, get so sore-footed that shoes are indispensable. The road is very hard and firm and strewn all over it is a fine sharp, angular, flinty gravel very small, about the size of a pea, and the least friction causes it to act like a rasp upon the opposing surface. The camel has no shuffle in his gait, but lifts his feet perpendicularly from the ground and replaces them, without sliding, as a horse or other quadrupeds do. This, together with the coarsely granulated and yielding nature of his foot, which though very tough, like gutta percha, yields sufficiently without wearing off, enables them to travel continuously in a country where no other barefooted beast would last a week.

El Paso was reached on July 29, and Beale remarked about the manner in which the camel ate an unnamed thorny fruit-bearing scrub bush which grew in abundance in West Texas.

> The camels seem to like both the branches and fruit better than any other we have met with. Although the branches are covered with sharp thorns, larger and stronger than those which grow on the rose bush, the camel seizes them in his mouth and draws the limb through his teeth, rapidly stripping off the leaves and briars and eating both greedily. Sometimes they bite off branches of considerable size and eat them leisurely, with apparent great ease. Their strength of jaw and teeth seems uncommonly great, greater than in proportion to their size when compared with other brutes.

The party now moved westward along the 35th Parallel in what is today western New Mexico toward Arizona. On August 19, Beale had the following "camel note" in his diary:

> Our camels are doing well here, and seem as fat as when we left, and apparently in better order for the road. On leaving Albuquerque they were packed with an average of seven hundred pounds each; the largest carried nearly a thousand pounds and the others in proportion to their size and strength.

By September 19, Beale and party had approached the Little Colorado River in North Central Arizona and the animals had been

without water for thirty-six hours. Beale recorded a pitiful sight in his diary entry on this date:
> ... one of the most painful sights I ever witnessed was a group of them (mules) standing over a small barrel of water and trying to drink from the bung hole, and seemingly frantic with distress and eagerness to get at it. The camels appeared to view this proceeding with great contempt, and kept quietly browsing on the grass and bushes.

A little later on in the entry for the same day Beale remarked that "Six of them [camels] are worth half the mules we have, although we have good ones."

The Colorado River, the first deep water barrier faced on the trip, was reached on October 18. This was an anxious time for Beale because it had been reported that the camels could not swim. As happened on every other phase of the trip the camels did not let him down, and this is how Beale dramatically described this crucial point in the trip:
> The first camel brought down to the river's edge refused to take the water. Anxious, but not discouraged, I ordered another one to be brought down, one of the largest and finest; and only those who have felt so much anxiety for the success of an experiment can imagine my relief on seeing it take to the water, and swim boldly across the rapidly flowing stream. We then tied them, each one to the saddle of another, and without the slightest difficulties, in a short time swam them all to the opposite bank in gangs, five in a gang. To my delight, they not only swam with ease, but apparently with more strength than a horse or mule. As a matter of fact all twenty-five camels swam across successfully. However, two horses and ten mules were drowned in the attempt.

Once this formidable water barrier was out of the way, the party made good time across the Mohave Desert following the United States surveyor's trail to Los Angeles. When the Mohave River was reached, Beale detached two camels and sent them to Los Angeles; the rest of the party took the right fork to Beale's Ranch near Fort Tejon about forty miles south of Bakersfield, California.

The two camels which had been sent to Los Angeles arrived there on November 10, 1857, and remained two days as an exhibit for the local population before joining the rest of the herd at Beale's Ranch. These were two of Beale's prize animals and they had made the last stage of the trip from San Bernardino to Los Angeles, a distance of sixty-five miles, in eight hours. One of the animals had been ten days without water and had refused water when it was offered to him at Los Angeles.

While at Fort Tejon Beale sent several camels high up in the mountains on his ranch to test their ability to withstand cold. The camels proved their ability in this experiment also as they lived in two or three feet of snow and fattened and thrived during the test. On one occasion during a severe snowstorm a wagon load of supplies for the mountain camp became stuck in the snow. Four camels were sent to rescue the mule drawn wagon and succeeded in bringing the load through the ice and snow to the camp, thus completing a task that six strong mules were unable to do.

On January 6, 1858, Beale started back east in order to test the practicability of the road in the winter that he had surveyed the previous fall along the 35th Parallel. For the return trip Beale took with him twenty men and fourteen of the twenty-five camels that he had brought west. The remainder of the camels, eleven, were left at Beale's Ranch and at Fort Tejon. On his way back east Beale first went south through Los Angeles where he received much publicity and then set out for San Bernardino where he picked up a soldier escort to accompany him as far as the Colorado River. The winter phase of the camel experiment officially ended near Zuni, New Mexico, on February 21, 1858. The camels performed as well on the way back as they had on the initial trip. The fourteen animals that made the trek back east were returned to the camel corral at Camp Verde.

Lieutenant Beale made his official report on the camel experiment to Secretary of War Floyd during the summer of 1858. In his report to Congress and the President in December, 1858, Floyd stated, "The entire adaptation of camels to military operations on the plains may now be taken as demonstrated," and he recommended that Congress authorize the purchase of 1,000 more camels immediately. However, the Legislators by this time were so concerned with the issues of Secession and slavery that Floyd's recommendations were not acted upon. In 1859 and again in 1860 Floyd brought forth his recommendation, but as earlier, no action was taken. Soon the conflict between the North and South broke out and that sounded the death knell for the proposed United States Camel Corps.

The experiment with the camel in our Southwest and Far West as a military transport vehicle in 1857 through 1860 proved conclusively that they were superior to both the horse and mule as beasts of burden. Lieutenant Beale and Mr. Stacy in their diary entries during the trek west and Lieutenants Beale and Porter and Major Wayne in their official reports to Secretary of War Davis and later to Secretary of War Floyd pointed out the tremendous advantage that the camel had over his two transport rivals. A camel could carry almost twice the load of a mule or a horse. It would eat anything from greasewood to cactus and thrive on same. The manner in which they walked, lifting their feet perpendicular from the ground and then replacing them without sliding, meant that they did not stumble and could traverse the roughest terrain without injuring their feet. The camel had the ability to travel great distances in hot weather without water. It was immune to rattlesnake bites, and it had great endurance and could travel 10 to 12 hours a day, day after day with a heavy load. Camels do not stampede or panic; saddle or baggage sores healed quickly; it is fearless almost to a fault and could negotiate snow, mud, sand, and rock-strewn places better than either the horse or the mule. Inasmuch as camels live an average of from 15 to 20 years longer than horses or mules, they were a more economical investment and they were docile, obedient, patient and immune to seasickness.

Even with these proven advantages over the horse and the mule the camel experiment failed. It was a tactical success but a strategic failure. This failure was principally due to the Civil War, which, of course, erased evereything else from the government's mind except the prosecution of the War itself. Also the two principal inhabitants of the Southwest at the time, the ranchers and the prospectors, were not particularly taken with the camels because they frightened their horses, cattle, and mules. The mule drivers also fought the introduction of the camel because it was a competitor that could put them out of business. Soon after the Civil War was over the Trans-Continental Railroad was built, and that made the use of the camel as a transport link with the Coast obsolete. Too, the aftermath of the Civil War was no different from the period following all of our wars prior to World War II, an accelerated demobilization, a parsimonious budget and a reluctance to think about anything military. All this added up to the failure of a successful experiment, unfortunately an oft-repeated phrase in American military history.

Thus ends the story of one of Jefferson Davis' fondest dreams. Nothing remains of it today but parched bones on the desert and a few graves in the Southwest to mark the failure of the attempt to establish a United States Camel Corps. His other dream, the independence of the Southern States, was also shattered and is marked today by crumbling tombstones in national cemeteries and parks. Thus passed into history two very interesting experiments in mid-nineteenth century America that ultimately failed, although both at one time came very close to succeeding.

There is an interesting epilogue to this story. Soon after Texas left the Union in early March, 1861, the Confederates took over Camp Verde including the some sixty camels still remaining there. The Confederate government used the camels for a short time to carry mail and supplies between their Texas outposts. However, they let the camel station deteriorate and the herd received little attention from the officers and soldiers. Early in 1863 three of the Camp Verde herd wandered away and were captured by the Union Army and sent north to Iowa. In June, 1863, the Missouri Military Department, which included the State of Iowa, asked the War Department for instructions concerning the disposition of the captured camels. Orders were issued to sell them at public auction which was done during the summer of 1863. No doubt other camels escaped from the Confederates at Camp Verde and wandered off through the wastelands of Texas, for ranchers and soldiers frequently saw them wandering wild through this area during the war years.

We know that the Confederate government brought at least one of the camels to the Gulf States during the War for it was reported in 1863 that a plowing contest was held in Montgomery, Alabama, between a mule and a camel. "It was a spirited and exciting contest for the numerous onlookers," the paper reported, and the results were decidedly in favor of the camel, although the paper added, "whether or not it [the camel] is more serviceable for the plantation purposes can hardly be decided yet." A captain on Confederate General Sterling Price's staff employed a camel to carry the headquarters baggage during the war, and a camel was reported to have carried the headquarters baggage of a Mississippi Regiment.

After Appomattox, Camp Verde and the camel herd which had propagated to a resounding sixty-six, again came under Federal control. On March 18, 1866, the Quartermaster at New Orleans received orders to sell the camels as soon as possible. The proposed sale was publicized, sealed bids were received, and the highest bid of $31.00 per head was accepted. The "hump-backed mules" were sold to a Colonel Bethal Coopwood of San Antonio who kept the herd near that city until December, 1866, when he made an unsuccessful attempt to start a camel caravan express between Laredo, Texas, and Mexico City. In January, 1867, the disillusioned Colonel started to dispose of his herd and eventually sold the animals to circuses, zoological gardens, and mining companies.

The other government-owned camels that were at Beale's Ranch had been turned over by Beale to the United States Quartermaster at Fort Tejon, California, in early 1861. In June, 1861, Fort Tejon was abandoned as an active military post and the herd was transferred to the United States Quartermaster at Los Angeles. Soon the camels were moved to San Pedro and were used to transport government supplies from that town to Los Angeles. In January, 1863, an attempt was made to use the camels for transportation between the army posts in southern California and those in Arizona, but it was unsuccessful and the idea was dropped. Finally in November, 1863, the Federal Government ordered the thirty-four animals of the San Pedro herd to the arsenal at Benicia, California, north of San Francisco. Capt. Depfill of the United States Army and six enlisted men conducted the camels to Benicia where they were sold at public auction on February 26, 1864. The entire herd of thirty-four camels was sold to a Samuel McLeneghan. McLeneghan sold three of his "ships of the desert" to Wilson's Circus which had its headquarters near Sacramento, California. On April 2, 1864, McLeneghan started a freight route between Sacramento and various settlements in the Nevada Territory. This venture soon proved to be uneconomical, and after the war those camels which had not been turned out or had escaped into the desert were sold to various mining interests in Nevada or to local circuses in California.

Thus ends the government's disposition of the seventy-five camels and their offspring that were imported into the United States for military purposes during 1856 and 1857. However, camels continued to be sighted in the deserts and mountains of our Southwest for many years after the war and even after the turn of the century. The last of the wild camels or their descendants was sighted as late as 1920 in the mountainous area of Western Arizona. Most of the animals that were turned free or that escaped into the wasteland were probably killed off by prospectors or ranchers who had developed an ingrained hatred for the beasts. Too, Apache Indians, who would eat anything that moved from snakes to cougars, probably accounted for quite a few of the unfortunate beasts. Of those government camels that found their way into circuses or midway shows the last known survivor was thought to be a U.S. branded Arabian sighted at a San Antonio midway show in May, 1903.

One interesting phase of this bizarre experiment remains to be told — the fate of the camel drivers and handlers (called cameleers) that were imported. All remained in the United States and eventually became American citizens. Three of them — "Long Tom," "Greek George," and "Hi-Jolly" had colorful careers and became legendary figures on the American scene. "Long Tom," an Arab driver, cared for the camel herd of the Ringling Brothers Circus for more than twenty-five years. "Greek George," who was actually a Syrian, was naturalized in Los Angeles County in 1866 as George Allen. Greek George was described as a modest, well-mannered, sturdy individual who possessed a tremendous beard and thatch of thick hair, so tangled and matted that it appeared bullet proof. As a matter of fact, in a fight with Indians near Camp Mohave an arrow struck him full in the jaw but barely penetrated his flesh through his massive beard. This quaint individual lived to an advanced age and died at Whittier, California on September 21, 1915.

Perhaps the best known and most colorful of the trio was another Syrian named "Hadja-Ali" whom the Americans soon anglicized to "Hi-Jolly." He was naturalized in California as Phillip Tedro, and prospected for gold for years around the Golden State calling San Bernardino his home. After his gold-panning days, Hi-Jolly acted as a guide and scout for the Army in Arizona. He reported wild camels in the region of the Gila and Colorado Rivers, and once saw a small herd of them in the tules of the Colorado just below the Mexican Border. Hi-Jolly was a flamboyant and unpredictable figure, and one story told about him concerned a large picnic given annually by the German Colony of Los Angeles to which he had not, but thought he should have, been invited. Suddenly in the midst of the "Deutschfesters" he appeared riding in a high yellow cart drawn by two large camels. It is said that the hills around the picnic grounds were strewn for weeks with beer bottles, bratwurst, cold schnitzel, broken halters and disabled vehicles. As in the case of the Texans, the Germans, as well as their horses, were allergic to camels. When Hi-Jolly died in 1903, he was buried in Quartzite, Arizona. The Arizona Highway Commission erected a suitable monument over his grave made from native rock with a copper camel on it. The plaque on the monument reads,

    THE LAST CAMP OF HI-JOLLY, BORN SOMEWHERE IN SYRIA ABOUT 1828, DIED AT QUARTZITE, DECEMBER 16, 1903. CAME TO THIS COUNTRY FEBRUARY 10, 1857. CAMEL DRIVER, PACKER, SCOUT. OVER 30 YEARS FAITHFUL SERVICE TO THE UNITED STATES GOVERNMENT.

A fourth driver must be mentioned, not particularly for his accomplishments, but for those of his son. Elias, another imported Syrian driver, after the camel herd was sold, migrated to Sonora, Mexico, where he eventually married a Yaqui Indian girl, settled down on a small rancho and raised a family. One of his sons, Plutarco Elias Calles, was president of Mexico from 1924 to 1928.

As a postscript to the Army's experiment with the "ships of the desert" was an even more bizarre idea which fortunately never materialized but was pondered long and hard by the top brass, including the Secretary of War in 1879. The idea discussed was the introduction of ostriches for use by United States Cavalry in the West. Yes,

CAMELS, JEFF DAVIS AND TEXAS

as strange as this idea may seem it almost bore fruit. An ostrich ranch of some 119 birds near Las Cucharas, New Mexico, had been singled out for the experiment. If the idea had been carried out, the Ninth United States Cavalry, a Black Regiment, was scheduled as the unit to receive the ostriches. The sight of the Buffalo Soldiers sitting among the feathers of their long-legged, long-necked, long-beaked mounts would probably have sent the Comanches into orbit.

BOOZE IN BATTLE AND BIVOUAC
THE DRINKING PROBLEM IN THE CIVIL WAR

GEN. U. S. GRANT
U.S.A.

GEN. JOSEPH HOOKER
U.S.A.

GEN. HENRY H. SIBLEY
C.S.A.

GEN. B. F. CHEATHAM
C.S.A.

FOUR GENERALS WHO HAD MORE THAN A NODDING
ACQUAINTANCE WITH JOHN BARLEYCORN.

BOOZE IN BATTLE AND BIVOUAC

> Just before the battle, Mother,
> I was drinking mountain dew.
> When I saw the Rebels marching
> To the rear I quickly flew.
> (A parody on George F. Root's immortal
> "Just Before the Battle, Mother")

Americans, as a whole, have been heavy drinkers from colonial times to the present day. As early as 1790 there were 1,500 grog shops in New York City alone or one saloon for about every fifty persons. Drinking was fashionable and common, if not universal. Rum, hard cider, and whiskey, to say nothing of beer and wine, were consumed in great quantities by both men and women. Liquor was served in prisons and at funerals. There was a statement that went the rounds of the London pubs in the early part of the 1800's that "a man could get drunk twice in America on six-pence."

Why this early thirst for the Demon Rum? Many historians give credit for this Bacchanalian debauchery to primitive and frontier conditions that existed in this nation in its early days. As a matter of fact, our frontier was not officially declared closed until 1890. Thus some 250 years of frontier living, with its hardships, its dangers, its lack of discipline and law and order, and the absence or scarcity of temporizing institutions made an indelible stamp upon the social mores of the American people.

Realizing that John Barleycorn, the proverbial name for ardent spirits, was getting a headlock on Uncle Sam's citizens, a number of prominent religious leaders in the 1820's and 30's led a nation-wide attempt to check intemperance. The Baptists and the Methodists, in particular, carried the cudgels to curb the imbibing culprits. The earliest non-alcoholic society of importance in the United States was "The Massachusetts Society for the Suppression of Intemperance" founded in 1813. During the next two decades the temperance movement made rapid progress. In 1826 "The American Society for the Promotion of Temperance" was organized at Boston, the city which appeared to be the stronghold of the prohibitionists, the teetotalers, and the blue noses. By 1833, there were some 6,000 local chapters of the Society and almost a million members. Other important temperance organizations founded before the Civil War included "The Washingtonian Movement" and "The Order of the Sons of Temperance." The former organization was said to have been launched by "six reformed drunkards of Baltimore" in the early 1840's and soon spread to hundreds of cities and towns throughout the country.

The pre-war temperance movement could be considered successful, not only because a great number of individuals took the pledge either to "cut down" or "lay off," but, because by 1860, thirteen states had passed prohibitionary laws against the manufacture and sale of spirituous beverages. Unfortunately, the many years of dedication and hard work of the tea sippers was largely negated, for the coming of the Civil War swept away the gains that had been made by the prohibitionists during the three previous decades.

Most of the young men who marched off to war after Fort Sumter had not been previously introduced to John Barleycorn. Generally the fuzzy-cheecked volunteers came from rural areas and from church oriented families. They had remained close to the family hearths, and a surprisingly large number had never traveled beyond the limits of their home counties. However, the bitterly fought, prolonged struggle between the North and the South with its privations, its dangers, and its lengthy periods of idleness produced ample opportunities for the teenagers to become addicted to the social liquid.

It was not uncommon for entire companies to publically swear abstinence before they left their home communities for the camps of instruction. This solemn oath, taken with good intentions, was often administered in the presence of the families and the ministers of the young recruits. Once free from the influence of the home and church, however, and in the company of older enlisted men and officers, many of whom openly cavorted with Bacchus, it was a different matter. For many the temptation was too great. Afraid not to be considered "one of the boys," they tried it and they liked it, and there lay the problem.

The late Bell I. Wiley, who, without a doubt, had read more letters written by Civil War soldiers than any other person, and who made an in-depth study of the wartime activities of the Northern and Southern soldiers, tells us that "excessive drinking was undoubtedly more common among Yanks than among Rebs." He then hastens to explain, however, that he didn't mean "that the Southerners were naturally more abstemious than their counterparts, but rather that they had less opportunity" to partake of booze in battle and bivouac. According to Wiley,

> intoxicants were more abundant in the North than in the Confederacy; Yanks had more money than Rebs and were more frequently stationed near large cities; whiskey was more often an item of government issue in the Northern armies; and the Federals had a more effective system of supply.

My research, however, has led me to believe that there was just as much imbibing by the soldiers from south of the Mason-Dixon line

★ ——————— BOOZE IN BATTLE AND BIVOUAC ——————— ★

as there was by those north of it. If the Confederates did not get whiskey as often and as easily as did the Federals, they appeared to have made more of the opportunities that came their way.

In order to discuss logically the subject of obfuscation, potation and tipsification in the armed forces during the Late Unpleasantness, it is necessary to break the elbow bending down into the following two logical parts: first, "Boozy Brigadiers, Snookered Surgeons and Other Commissioned Inebriates" and second, "Soused Sergeants, Crocked Corporals and Plastered Privates." Thus let us proceed with the officer corps first, as I believe they provide the best examples of recorded inebriation. Numerous generals who fought under both the Stars and Stripes and the Stars and Bars earned reputations during the war as tipplers of the tonic. To be sure several of the brass such as Ulysses Simpson Grant on the Federal side and Henry Hopkins Sibley on the Confederate side had pretty well embraced the habit long before the Civil War.

Grant had started to drink heavily while a company grade officer stationed on the West Coast in the early 1850's. He resigned from the Army in 1854 to avoid a court-martial for inebriation and other associated charges and then submerged from public life for seven years doing odd jobs in Missouri and Illinois. Finally he emerged from oblivion after Fort Sumter. The War gave Grant a new lease on life, and he rose rapidly from Colonel of the 21st Illinois Infantry Regiment to Lieutenant-General in command of all the Federal armies in the field. It was no secret that one of Colonel John A. Rawlins's principal duties as the General's Chief of Staff was to keep Ulysses Grant and John Barleycorn from fraternizing. Rawlins appears to have done a commendable job, although the General was reported to have been drinking both at Shiloh and Vicksburg. According to the Colonel, Grant switched from bourbon to wine about mid-way through the war and then finally turned to cigars which eventually killed him. Thus, it appears, at least in the case of Grant, that Burley is more deadly than Bourbon.

Lincoln was well aware of his military commander's weakness but constantly joked about it. On one occasion the Great Emancipator was approached by a delegation headed by a distinguished doctor of divinity who had come down from New York to complain about Grant's bourbonizing. After the man of the cloth had concluded his remarks, Lincoln, looking as serious as he could under the circumstances, said, "Doctor, can you tell me where General Grant gets his liquor?" The Reverend with a puzzled look on his face replied that he could not. The President then said to him, "I am sorry, for if you could tell me I would direct the Quartermaster-General of the Army to lay in a large stock of the same kind of liquor, and would also direct him to furnish a supply to some of my generals who have never yet won a victory."

"Fighting Joe" Hooker (whose name rhymes with snooker), the handsome Federal general whom Lincoln entrusted, against his better judgment, with the command of the Army of the Potomac for the first half of 1863, was not known as a teetotaler. As a matter of fact his vices ran the gamut from gambling to girls, but we are concerned at this time only with his proclivity for strong potation. Historians are still not certain what happened to Joe Hooker at Chancellorsville where he commanded the Federals' futile efforts to corral Marse Bob Lee. At the height of the engagement, while standing on the porch of the Chancellor House, Hooker suddenly collapsed leaving his senior corps commander, Darius Nash Couch, to direct operations. Some observers reported that Fighting Joe had been nipping of the nectar that fateful day at Chancellorsville to screw up his courage in the face of the challenge by Lee. On the other hand, his staff stoutly maintained that Fighting Joe was felled by a chunk of wood split from a porch column (upon which he was leaning) by a Confederate cannon ball. Regardless, the stunned or stoned or snookered Hooker was carried from the field in a horizontal position and ended up far behind the lines in a stupor, while has army stampeded back across the Rappahannock, just a tad behind their fearless leader.

According to my good friend Wally Hebert, Hooker's biographer, "the General's personal habits have been the subject of much debate. His close followers were ever ready to testify that they had never seen him take a drink but current nonpartisan opinion held otherwise." Eventually a parody was developed on the popular war time hit "Marching Along." The lines

> "McClellan's our leader,
> He's gallant and strong."

were replaced by

> "Joe Hooker's our leader,
> He takes his whiskey strong."

Francis A. Lord in his *Civil War Sutlers and their Wares* states that "at the headquarters of such generals as Hooker and Burnside there was ample evidence of liberal indulgence in all kinds of intoxicants. The list is almost endless; champagne, ale, and whiskey were probably the most popular.

Grant and Hooker, of course, were not alone among the Federal military leaders addicted to alcohol. Brigadier General James Totten,

★——————— BOOZE IN BATTLE AND BIVOUAC ———————★

a hard boiled West Pointer, was said always to have gone into action with a canteen full of brandy at his hip. Due to his fondness of drink, Totten acquired the nickname, "Bottle-nosed Totten." The boozing brigadier was finally dismissed from the army after the war for "excessive drinking." Perhaps the most disgraceful conduct of an inebriated Union general officer occurred during the battle of the Crater at Petersburg in July of 1864. Brigadier General James Hewitt Ledlie, who was in command of the assault division following the unsuccessful mine explosion, failed to go forward with his men. He was discovered following the futile attack "snugly tucked away in a bombproof, 400 yards behind the lines, plying himself with rum borrowed from a brigade surgeon." Phil Sheridan, the tough, diminutive and bow-legged Federal cavalry leader, carried a silver flask that saw continuous action (elbow action that is) during the fratricidal fracas, and General Judson Kilpatrick, also of the Federal mounted service, was reported as carousing several times during the war. It was difficult to deteremine which "Kill Cavalry" Kilpatrick had the greatest affinity for — whiskey or women.

Bruce Catton in his *Glory Road*, a partial history of the Army of the Potomac, tells a humorous story of a distinguished general of the VI Corps of that famous Army. It appears that this brigadier, whom Catton fails to identify, had too much to drink one evening at one of the Corps' frequent blowouts. The General left the party in a mellow mood full of sympathy for his orderly who had been standing out in the cold all evening holding the brigadier's horse. Catton continues with the story,

> The brigadier took his bridle reins and teetered gently on his heels and remarked to the orderly: "Do you know, I'd like to take a drink with you." Then sadly he added that this just would not do because there was a great gulf between them. "You're an orderly, sir, and I'm a general, sir; recollect that, sir." The orderly swayed in the dim light, exhaling an aroma fully as fruity as that of the brigadier's and replied: "By george, General, hadn't you better wait til you're asked."

It appears, however, that the Confederate Brass were a little more proficient in the bending of the elbows than were their Northern counterparts. H. H. Sibley, previously mentioned and an inventor of note and a boozer of consequence while in the Old Army on frontier duty in Texas, continued his guzzling habits while serving under the St. Andrews Cross. His condition was highly suspect during the New Mexico Campaign of 1861-62, and at least twice later in the war he was detained and questioned for his "alleged predilection for the bottle."

"Price John" Magruder, commander of the District of Texas, New Mexico and Arizona for a good part of the conflict, kept an open bar in his Galveston quarters where he lavishly entertained civilians as well as military personnel. The parties that Magruder gave were such Bacchanalian affairs and epicurean delights, that on one occasion at least, the debauchery triggered a mutiny by the Galveston garrison who had little to eat and nothing to drink.

Nathan G. "Shanks" Evans, the garrulous commander of the "Tramp Brigade," was tried twice for a combination of "drunkenness and disobedience" and, although acquitted both times, was later deprived of his command by Beauregard for incompetence — the charge against Shanks no doubt being triggered by his love for liquor. Tom Rosser, George B. Crittenden, Earl Van Dorn, John B. Villepique, John C. Breckinridge, and Theophilus Hunter Holmes, at various times, were said to have been drunk either in bivouac or battle or both. *Harper's Weekly* of August 29, 1863, reported that the last named "had died recently of delirium tremens." This report, of course, was false as Holmes lived until 1880.

Benjamin Franklin Cheatham was a nipper of note. He reportedly could "outcurse any man in his division" and apparently could also outdrink any man in his command of Tennesseans. Braxton Bragg reported that "in the battle of Murfreesboro, Cheatham was so drunk on the field all the first day, that a staff officer had to hold him on his horse." Cheatham took the alternate name for the battle of Murfreesboro, Stone's River, too literally and, as Bragg observed, was reported to have been stoned at the battle by a lieutenant in Company K of the 6th Tennessee Infantry Regiment. The lieutenant told a friend that

> . . . at the beginning of the battle [of Murfreesboro] while his troops were standing in line waiting for orders to move, General Cheatham rode out in front and in attempting to wave his hat to make an appeal to his "Tennesseans" rolled off his horse and fell to the ground as limp and helpless as a bag of meal — to the great humiliation and mortification of his troops.

William J. Hardee had also reported Cheatham, a division commander in his corps later in the war, drunk on several occasions. At the Confederate debacle at Spring Hill, in the fall of 1864, Cheatham was accused of being drunk in bed, allowing Schofield's Federal army to pass by unscathed to Franklin and victory. There is some reason to believe that the General may have been sharing his bed with the delectable Mrs. George B. Peters who had caused the early demise of Earl Van Dorn for the same reason a few months previously.

John O. Casler of the Stonewall Brigade told the following story on General Arnold Elzey:

> General Elzey was quite fond of a dram, as most soldiers are, and one night when he and his staff were drinking quite freely, and feeling very liberal, he called in the sentinel who was on guard at his quarters and gave him a drink, and then went to bed. Now, when this same sentinel was on post again, about daylight, he put his head in the tent door, and finding the General still asleep, woke him up by exclaiming: "General! General!, ain't it about time for us to take another drink?" The General roused up, and not being in as merry a mood as the night before, ordered him to be taken off to the guard house for his insolence. That soldier was greeted for months afterwards by the whole command with the refrain, "General! General!, ain't it time for us to take another drink?"

Two general officers who wore the grey and who were associated with the Texas Brigade in Virginia — W. H. C. Whiting and Louis T. Wigfall — were heavy drinkers both off and on duty. The Texas Brigade served in Whiting's division during the winter and spring of 1862. Whiting, a brilliant student, graduating first in his class at West Point, and an engineering officer in the United States Army prior to the Southern exodus, "brooded over his failure to play a role in the war commensurate with his talents" and apparently turned to drink and narcotics to sooth his wounded pride. Joe Joskins, a member of the 5th Texas Infantry of Hood's Brigade, while on guard duty one night at Whiting's Headquarters reported the General "a little boozy" when he stammered out to a fellow officer, "There's nobody worth a damn but myself and the Texas Brigade." Whiting was accused of being "under the influence of whisky or narcotics" during the summer of 1864 at Petersburg and was subsequently transferred to Fort Fisher, North Carolina where early in 1865 he was mortally wounded.

Louis Trezevant Wigfall, bombastic and booze-addict commander of the Texas Brigade in Virginia was a devotee of strong drink — hard cider being his special delight. "Wiggletail," as Sam Houston referred to him, kept a bottle of aged applejack conveniently jugged at the foot of his cot and nipped on it at frequent intervals causing noctural hallucinations and visions of hordes of Federals swooping down upon his brigade. On numerous occasions during the fall and winter of 1861, the jittery general called his brigade out in the middle of the night "to repel a major Yankee invasion" — invasions that turned out to be nothing more than a few Federal scouts lurking in the area. After two or three of these false alarms, regimental commanders John B. Hood and James J. Archer refused to call their men out when the long roll sounded.

J. B. Polley, the historian of the Texas Brigade, reported that Wigfall appeared drunk in front of his troops on more than one occasion. Eugene O. Perry of the First Texas Infantry wrote home that the General was "on a little bender," and young Robert Gaston of the same regiment said in a letter to his parents that General Wigfall had "one great fault. He loves whiskey too well. He has been drunk several times since we came here." True to form, when Wigfall moved his regiment from Manassas to Dumfries in the fall of 1861, he established his headquarters in the "little village tavern" there. Fortunately for the Texas Brigade the befuddled brigadier never had to lead them in battle. He was appointed to the Confederate Senate by the Texas Legislature in winter of 1861-62 where he proceeded to become a thorn in the side of Jefferson Davis.

Stonewall Jackson, Lee's great lieutenant who was famous for his puritanic habits, I am sorry to have to report, did upon occasion drink spirituous liquids. Following the Fredericksburg campaign in the winter of 1862-63, Jackson became chilled one evening and "drank freely" from a bottle presented to him by an admirer. According to one of his aides.

> When he had consumed about half of it, he passed the bottle among his staff .... Within a few moments, as they rode toward the enemy, Jackson began a most unnatural chattering. Sweat appeared on his face, and despite the cold air, he unfastened his coat garrulously discussing a variety of subjects. Jackson, was for the only recorded time in his life, half drunk.

On yet another occasion, while having dinner with his lieutenants Jackson poured an oversized drink and downed it at a gulp much to the amazement of his staff. He had done this by design. He then lectured to his staff and told them that he differed with them and most men. "I like the taste of spirituous liquor," said Jackson. "I can sip whiskey or brandy with a spoon with the same pleasure the most delicious coffee or cordial would give you. I am the fondest man of liquor in the army," continued the famous general, "and if I had indulged my appetite, I would have been a drunkard. But liquors are not good for me .... At any rate I rarely touch them."

Jackson admitted to Colonel A. R. Boteler early in the War, that he abstained from drinking liquor because he liked "the taste of it so much" and when he "found that out [he] made up his mind to do without it." It is too bad that some of the other generals did not have the self-discipline of Old Jack. A few battles might have had a different outcome.

A colonel in his cups assigned to the Sixteenth Wisconsin Infantry lay down on the firing line with the privates and commenced shooting at the enemy. When the soldier next to him asked the Colonel how many Rebels he had shot, the bleary-eyed officer, pausing an unusually long time to ponder the question and then recollecting carefully, said that "he had fired thirty-seven cartridges and so, of course, should have hit thirty-seven men but did not feel certain of six."

The First New York Infantry, composed of "Bowery Boys" from New York City, "was officered by misfits," reported Francis A. Lord. Illustrative of the lax leadership of this regiment was an itemized bill of 1861, listing medical stores for the month of April. Among the "medicines" and "pharmaceutical" items listed were:

120 gallons of bourbon whiskey
42 gallons of pale sherry
21½ gallons of pale otard brandy
40 gallons of cabinet gin (and)
24 dozen bottles of Allsop East India Ale

The colonel of this illustrious unit was cashiered from the service before the year was out.

And then there is the humorous story of Lieutenant Alonzo Chubb of Company D, 105th Ohio Infantry Regiment. Usually when one asks for "two fingers of whiskey" he is referring to an amount that would fill an average size shot glass but not Chubb. The Lieutenant, who had lost the two middle fingers of one hand, when asked to imbibe would place his hand with only the first and little finger on it beside the glass and say, "Only two fingers, if you please!" and thus would get twice as much whiskey as a four-fingered fellow. Chubb was captured by the Confederates near Murfreesboro, Tennessee, on January 21, 1863, and was sent by train from Atlanta to Richmond along with a group of other Yankee prisoners. The commander of the guard detail was a congenial Confederate captain who was so enamored by Chubb's joke that he took the Lieutenant off the train "at every station where they stopped long enough to visit a saloon, to show the Yankee method of measuring a drink." The poor quality of whiskey available in the Confederacy made this a trying ordeal for the Federal Lieutenant, but just the same "the favor shown to Chubb greatly excited the envy of his fellow prisoners of war."

Naturally during the holiday times drinking was more prevalent. Private Sam Watkins of the 1st Tennessee Infantry Regiment writing after the war recalled, "It was Christmas. John Barleycorn was general-in-chief. Our generals, and colonels, and captains, had kissed John a little too often. They couldn't tell our own men from the Yankees."

It was a hard drinking war as far as the officers on both sides were concerned. "Any [Northern] officer," Bruce Catton wrote, "could legally buy all of the whiskey he thought that he could handle from the commissary stores." According to Catton, the commissary whiskey was "cheap and reliable," however, when the original supply was exhausted, the issue was "raw and harsh" although it still remained cheap. "Some officers," Catton continued,
> would simmer it over a fire in order to reduce the harshness; others believed in setting fire to it and letting it burn awhile, arguing that this destroyed the fusel oil and other harmful substances. However they treated it, they used a good deal of it, and soldier's sleep was occasionally disturbed by singing and yelling from the officer's quarters. Colonel Cross of the 5th New Hampshire broke up one such party in his own regiment by stalking in with his drawn sabre in one hand a pair of handcuffs in the other.

According to George W. Adams, author of *Doctors in Blue*, "Alcohol was the sovereign remedy of the Civil War, rivalled only by quinine." It was prescribed by the medical officers for everything imaginable from "bites of rattlesnakes" to use as a "prophylactic against the influence of morning dews." Bourbon was consumed to combat malaria, as a substitute for brackish drinking water, as a stimulant after "periods of unusual exposure to dampness or of excessive hardship," to "counteract shock" and as an "appetizer for convalescents." Beer was recommended by some army surgeons as being good for both the bladder and bowels — and I guess that we cannot argue with that, particularly in regard to the former. The Germans were particularly fond of the amber liquid, and Fred Shannon, in his *Organization and Administration of the Union Army*, reported that in some German-American companies in the Federal army it was customary "to have from two to a dozen barrels of lager beer on hand."

Unfortunately, many of the doctors who wore the Blue and the Gray were not satisfied merely to recommend alcoholic stimulants for the use of others but prescribed large dosages for themselves. Phoebe Pember, a matron at Chimborazo, the large Confederate hospital on the outskirts of Richmond, stated in her reminiscences, that "there was some doubt afloat as to whether the benefit conferred upon the patients by the use of stimulants counterbalanced the evil effects they produced on the surgeons." "Drunkenness," wrote George Adams, "was the commonest charge against the surgeons," and "many surgeons," reported a Southern war correspondent, "when engaged at the amputation table [felt] it to be their solemn duty everytime that they administered brandy to the patient to take a drink themselves."

There is no doubt that the easy access to liquor caused some of the medical personnel to lean too heavily upon the bottle. At Fort

Donelson the senior medical officer of the 52nd Indiana Infantry Regiment was "drunk for a 24-hour period." The inebriated surgeon of an Ohio regiment abandoned 53 sick men of his unit in the winter of 1862 without a change of clothing, medicine, food, or blankets enough to keep them from freezing, and headed north with his wife. A report from a Federal hospital concerning an amputation case stated that the patient bled to death because the surgeon operating "was too drunk to take up the arteries."

On the other side of the lines, H. H. Cunningham, in his *Doctors in Gray*, reported similar incidents among the Confederate medical personnel. "Surgeons in the field," wrote Cunningham, "were sometimes reported to be in a state of intoxication even during the course of an engagement." During the Atlanta Campaign an assistant surgeon in the Army of Tennessee was dismissed from the service "for habitual drunkenness while on duty and for leaving his command and abandoning the sick and wounded men of his regiment while on an active campaign and in the face of the enemy." At Chimborazo Hospital a soldier was brought in whose ankle had been crushed in a railroad accident. While he was still in shock his leg was placed in a cast by a drunken surgeon and his assistants, and only hours later when the man complained of intense pain in his "good" leg was it discovered that the wrong leg had been set. A war correspondent for a Richmond paper, near the end of the war, wrote, "that he had seen surgeons so stupified by liquor that they could not distinguish between a man's arm and the spoke of a wagon wheel, and who would have just as soon sawed off the one as the other."

Fortunately most of the surgeons remained sober, but there were enough who habitually imbibed to make amputating and operating a rather sporting proposition, particularly for the patient.

Now on to some stories about soused sergeants, crocked corporals and plastered privates. Although the non-commissioned officers and privates were not entitled either to buy or draw spirituous beverages from the commissary stores, except by permission of their commanding officers and the regimental surgeons, somehow, someway, they managed to secure enough firewater to engage in some real rip-snorters. Several mass drinking orgies have been recorded and credited to inebriated enlistees. One of the most publicized of these drinking bouts, occurred in the Federal Army while en route to the battle of Gettysburg.

Edwin B. Coddington in his fine work, The *Gettysburg Campaign,* gives a vivid description of the "sacking of Frederick, Maryland" by Meade's Army as it passed through on June 28, 1863, on the march to Pennsylvania. After months of campaigning in war-scarred Virginia and perhaps a little fearful of facing Robert E. Lee again, the boys in Blue turned this sleepy Maryland town into a Falstaffian fiesta. The inhabitants of Frederick, however, are somewhat to blame for what happened. In their joy to see the Federal Army, they "greeted the soldiers with open arms" and Sunday, June 28, "became a festive and memorable occasion when business in stores and saloons went on as usual even while churches were open for worship." Many of the soldiers "wound up in the bars where good Maryland rye whiskey was plentiful." To compound the problem at Frederick in late June 1863, the Army of the Potomac had, just prior to the junket into Pennsylvania, undergone a change of commanders, Meade replacing Hooker, with the result that some confusion existed in the administration of orders. Too, General Marsena Patrick, the Provost-Marshal General, had no cavalry detachment at his disposal with which to enforce and maintain discipline. Thus, the ingredients were present for the rum and rye rampage that resulted.

Eyewitnesses have left a picture of the "pandemonium" that engulfed Frederick "for several days."

> Scores of inebriated officers and soldiers made the nights hideous, reeling down the streets, trying to steal horses or break into houses, and "filling the air with the blasphemy of their drunken brawls." During the day "hundreds" of men were sleeping it off, "lying about the streets, on the door steps, under fences, in the mud, dead drunk." The attractions of Frederick produced an undue amount of straggling in every corps of the army. From there on north, the road was said to be "lined" with stragglers, and every farm was overrun with drunken soldiers, who swarmed around the stables and stole horses whenever they could to avoid walking. Others wheedled or frightened women into giving them food and lodging. In fence corners along the road groups lay too drunk to get up. The few patrols that went out to gather up stragglers were "ineffective," and many of them were drunk too. Even some unusually conscientious soldiers who after days of hard marching had sought a little relaxation and indulged too heavily in the bottle could not keep up with their regiments and fell by the wayside.

General Henry W. Slocum, commander of the Twelfth Corps of the Federal Army, sent Meade a dispatch saying that when he left Frederick there were a "great number of men from every corps lying about the streets beastly drunk."

Hood's Texans engaged in a notable drinking spree when the Brigade was en route by train from Richmond to Atlanta to participate in the Chickamauga affair. During the train ride to Georgia, the Brigade had a twenty-four hour layover in Wilmington, North Carolina. With time on their hands, a group of the Texans engaged in a spirited drinking bout in an unsavory waterfront section of the port city known as "Paddy's Hollow." With the aroma of schnapps and hops about them, the Lone Star Staters became boisterous, obnoxious and abusive. The night police force consisting of a half dozen elderly citizens of Wilmington were hastily summoned to corral the noisemakers. The Texans peering through bloodshot eyes apparently mistook the blue uniformed lawmen for Yankees, for they immediately formed a battle line, raised the Rebel Yell, and staggered to the charge. One constable said to be in his late fifites was badly beaten about the face, another was knocked down by a shillelagh blow over the ear, while a third police officer suffered two knife wounds in his side. The pommeled nocturnal guardians limped to a hasty retreat carrying their wounded with them and left the waterfront to the Lone Star victors.

One mass drinking bout during the war, among the many preserved for posterity by Civil War writers and in soldier's letters, was quite unexpected and most unusual. The 48th New York Infantry Regiment, commanded by the prominent minister, the Reverend James M. Perry, and known as "Perry's Saints," had all taken the abstinence pledge prior to leaving the state. Unfortunately for the reputation of the regiment, during June of 1862, while the unit was stationed on Tybee Island, Georgia, a storm blew ashore a large supply of beer and wine which Perry's Saints promptly commandeered and then proceeded to drink down and get roaring drunk. Unable to cope with this mass backsliding from abstinence to alcoholism, and his dream of commanding the only sober regiment in the Federal Army shattered, the Colonel collapsed at his desk from a heart attack and died the following day.

According to E. Merton Coulter, whiskey was readily available "in almost every town and hamlet" in the South and "it easily found its way into the army." Most of it consisted of concoctions that one would not even gargle with, let alone drink, in time of peace. Its effects were often described in humorously exaggerated language. A Macon, Georgia editor reached the heights of absurdity in writing that the liquid passing for whiskey

> would conglomerate the vesicles of the aorta, phlogistify the phylacter maximus, hemstitch up the hepatic ducts, insulate the asperifollus gland, deflagrate the dudonian process, and wilt the buttons off the waistcoat, besides doing a good many other things which might be too tedious to specify.

Bell Wiley, who, as previously noted had made a career out of collating soldiers' letters, wrote that most of the whiskey consumed during the conflict was composed of only "about thirty per cent genuine alcohol, and the rest [being] made up with water, vitriol, and coloring matter. An old and mellow taste [was] secured by adding the raw flesh of wild game, or young veal or lamb . . . [and] soaking for three or four weeks."

Alcoholic spirits were referred to by many terms. In a religious tract circulated among the Confederate soldiers by the army chaplains, it was called "distilled damnation." Governor Brown of Georgia, a vehement teetotaler and Baptist deacon, in March of 1862 issued a proclamation forbidding the use of corn in making what he described as that "burning liquid stream of death, which is spreading desolation and ruin throughout the whole length and breadth of the land." Soldiers referred to the social liquid as "how come you so," "oil of gladness," "tanglefoot," "the ardent," "Oh be joyful," "turpentine," "brown sugar," "nockum stiff," "bark juice," "tar-water," "red eye," "rot gut," "pop skull," "bust head," "rifle knock-knee," and "lamp-oil," among other things.

The hope of every soldier was to visit Washington or Richmond as often as possible, there to get drunk, attend the theater, and seek feminine company. Soldiers drank and fought one another and civilians on the streets, broke open saloons on Sundays, visited the markets and slashed watermelons with their bowie knives or tossed them into the air and caught them on their bayonets. In order to win a bet, a soldier (undoubtedly intoxicated) smashed a thick plate glass window in the American Hotel in Richmond with his fist. Drunken soldiers killed civilians, and in turn were killed by civilians. The Richmond *Examiner* reported on June 9, 1862, that "upwards of a dozen drunken soldiers were knocked down in the streets and robbed the previous Saturday night." Earlier in this same year (1862) the paper had observed: "one only has to go into the streets of the city [at night] to see hundreds of good looking men wearing the uniform of their country's service, imbruted by liquor, converted into barroom vagabonds."

Although it is hard to conceive of, at times there was a whiskey shortage in certain localities. It was facetiously asserted on such rare occasions that men were "cutting off their mustachios to keep from losing a tenth part of every drink by capillary attraction."

As time passed and stricter controls were exercised over the transportation of spirituous beverages into camp, Johnny Reb, Billy Yank and the sutlers on both sides came up with ingenious methods of hoodwinking the provost guards and camp inspectors. Loaves of bread were hollowed out to smuggle in bottles of liquor, and demijohns of strong drink were frequently concealed in loads of stable manure. Watermelons, cantaloupes, and pumpkins had the centers cut out and were filled with bourbon, wine and brandy. Half-pint bottles were hidden in pies and cakes, and larger containers of liquid damnation were smuggled in by means of cases marked "boots and shoes" and "preserved fruit." On one occasion, according to Francis A. Lord, a woman was apprehended "with about five gallons of whiskey suspended in canteens from her belt and in bottles in a number of pockets." Women peddlers were discovered smuggling whiskey into a Federal camp in Texas by hiding it "under their clothes and in their bosoms."

John O. Casler of the Stonewall Brigade reported that he and his messmates purchased a keg of whiskey from a sutler on the sly "and smuggled it into the tent and buried it in the ground under the bunk," from which it was ladled out from time to time.

Fred Shannon, an authority on the organization of the Union Army, gives the following description of an original method of smuggling used by a New York vendor in the summer of 1863.

> A regiment of soldiers arriving, too late to help in suppressing the New York City draft riots, was stationed on Governor's Island, New York, pending developments. Being cut off from the mainland, many were parching under the liquor restrictions. Then a benefactress come to them in the shape of an old woman selling sausages. To the men who had been living on salt and smoked meat for so long a time, the idea of sausage was repellent. Consequently sales seemed likely to be very small until a whispered communication brightened up the faces of the men and the sausages were sold in a hurry. The skins were filled not with sausage meat but with bourbon whiskey.

Wiley tells of members of a Mississippi company who smuggled a half-gallon of liquor into camp in a hollowed-out watermelon, hid it beneath the floor of their tent, and "tapped it with a long straw. When one of them wanted a drink," continued Wiley, "he lay flat on the floor and sucked the straw." To make sure tht all received an equal amount, "his comrades stood by to cut him off after his Adam's apple registered his ration of two swallows." But the most daring strategem of all," reported Wiley,

> Was attributed to an Irishman of the 2nd Tennessee Volunteers. The Colonel of this outfit while walking through camp one day saw Pat elevate his gun and take a long pull at the muzzle. He called out, "Pat, what have you got in your gun?" Came back the answer, "Colonel, Sir, I was looking at the barrel of my gun to see whether she was clean." And after the unwary officer walked on the Irishman completed draining his gun barrel of the whiskey thus smuggled in from a nearby town.

The holiday season always set off a series of drinking sprees. Few soldiers' diaries, letters home and reminiscences fail to mention the indulgence in toddies and other spirits on Christmas Day and New Year's Eve. While most of these celebrations were probably nothing more than congenial social affairs among a small party of friends, some, of course, got out of hand and developed into real Donnybrooks. Sergeant Onley Andrus of the 95th Illinois Infantry Regiment reported one such a Bacchanalian affair that occurred on Christmas Day, 1864. According to Andrus, the regimental commander "turned out 15 gallons of rotgut and several of the boys got happy, and some got pugilistic, and as a consequence some had eyes red and some black and all felt as though they had been poorly staid at best."

An even more riotous affair was reported by a sergeant who related his experiences at a New Year's Eve party held by a New Jersey regiment.

> Last night I had plenty of whiskey but today I have none, we had five canteens full and we had a merry old time. They broke all my furniture, tore my table cloth and turned everything upside down. I thought I would fire a salute. I got my musket and fired it, and I set my tent afire and by the time I got through, my tent was most burnt up. New Year's don't come but once a year and tents are cheap.

Punishment meted out for ordinary drunkenness varied with the commander. A captain in charge of an artillery company tied the boozers in his battery "by the hand to the rear of a gun (and doused them in the face with a bucket of water from time to time) so as to insure their keeping up." An infantry colonel, "to make the punishment symbolical," clothed the culprit concerned "in a barrel with only his head, legs, and arms sticking out while bearing some label [such] as 'Too fond of whiskey' or 'Forged an order on the surgeon'." In another case the inebriates were tied to a stake and had to remain out in the sun, rain or snow for a twelve hour period. The colonel of the 150th Pennsylvania Infantry Regiment sentenced three drunks in his regiment "to walk in barrels for six days for continuous drunkenness." A soldier in another Pennsylvania regiment, found drunk on duty, "was compelled to carry a musket and a carpet bag strapped to his back containing fifty pounds of stones."

If the case of drunkenness was of a more serious nature the punishment, of course, was more severe. A Confederate private found in the arms of John Barleycorn while guarding prisoners at Tullahoma, Tennessee, in January, 1863, "was required to stand on the head of a barrel with a whiskey bottle hanging from his neck for two hours each day for a month, and while not thus enaged to do hard labor." Then there is the case of Sergeant Jules Freret and Corporal Gustave Aime, who while in their cups made the mistake of "demanding a drink of their captain and then proceeding to cut the rope of his tent when refused. The two were given courts-martial sentences of reduction of rank, fifteen turns of guard duty, and thirty days confinement to camp."

Although leaders on both sides condemned and decried the use of intoxicants, it appeared to have little effect on the troops. Generals Braxton Bragg and George B. McClellan, both noted blue-nosers, led the fight against the use of whiskey and its demoralizing effects. Bragg claimed that "over half of the courts-martial cases in his army rose out of drunkenness" and complained that "his army had lost more valuable lives at the hands of the whiskey sellers than by the ball of the enemy." McClellan stated in February, 1862,

> No one evil agent so much obstructs this army . . . as the degrading vice of drunkenness. It is the cause of by far the greater part of the disorders which are examined by courts-martial. It is impossible to estimate the benefits that would accrue to the service from the adoption of a resolution on the part of officers to set their men an example to total abstinence from intoxicating liquors. It would be worth 50,000 men to the armies of the United States.

While it is probably true that the great majority of the officers and the enlisted men in both armies were sober and upright men, there is no doubt that drinking was a major problem during the fratricidal fracas. Paraphrasing the well-known story of Virginia and Santa Claus, I conclude my presentation with — Yes, my friends, during the Late Unpleasantness there was a John Barleycorn, and he did rub shoulders in bivouac and battle with Johnny Reb and Billy Yank and without regard to rank or grade.

LEE WEST OF THE RIVER
ROBERT E. LEE IN MISSOURI, MEXICO & TEXAS

— NATIONAL ARCHIVES

LIEUTENANT ROBERT E. LEE, 1831
U.S. CORPS OF ENGINEERS

AFTER A PAINTING CREDITED TO BENJAMIN WEST, JR.

LEE WEST OF THE RIVER

The subject of my presentation needs no introduction to this audience. Probably no military leader is more revered in the United States than is Robert E. Lee. In the South, which has provided this country with many leaders from George Washington to George Patton, Lee is regarded as a patron saint. As a general, he has had few, if any, equals in American History and his private life was without blemish and above reproach. Military prowess and purity of habits are not often found in tandem, but Robert E. Lee fit this mold. He had no vices and was a gentleman of the highest order. Douglas Southall Freeman, who had examined all of Lee's correspondence when writing his superb award winning definitive biography of the General, stated "His [Lee's] entire correspondence does not contain the echo of liaison, the shadow of an oath, or the stain of a single obscene suggestion!"

During my military career I was stationed in several of the Southern states — Virginia, North Carolina, Alabama and Texas, a crescent from the Southeast to the Southwest. This has given me, a Midwesterner by birth and education, an unusual opportunity to see and study all sections of the South. (In fact, I regard myself a Southerner by osmosis). Almost without exception in the homes where I was a guest during these periods of Southern exposure, there hung on the wall or stood on a table a picture or a bust of Robert E. Lee. He was the idol of the Old South.

While attending the Air War College at Montgomery, Alabama in the late 1950's, I made the acquaintance of a well-known, elderly judge of that city — a man whose father, as a young officer on Lee's staff, had carried the flag of truce into the Union lines that fateful April 9, 1865. The Judge told me, during a period of reminiscing in his home one evening over a mint julep, of an elderly lady acquaintance of his who feeling the approach of death had sent for her pastor. As the man of the cloth sat by the bedside consoling her as her life ebbed away, she suddenly touched his hand, looked into his face with a soft smile and whispered that she was not afraid to die. "For I shall be in heaven," she said, "and there I shall be with the three men I have loved most; my Savior, my husband and Robert E. Lee." And that is how the old time Southerners thought of Lee.

There have been hundreds of books written on the life of Robert E. Lee. Most of them have emphasized his career with the Confederate Army. My presentation will concern itself primarily with a period in the life of this great Virginian and great American that is not so well known to the general public, his military assignments west of the Mississippi River. This will include three phases of his military career prior to the War Between the States, the years 1837-1840 when Lee served as an engineering officer stationed at St. Louis, Missouri; his participation in the Mexican War, 1846-1848; and the period when, as a lieutenant-colonel with the èlite Second United States Cavalry, he was stationed in Texas during the period 1855-1861. These assignments across the Mississippi account for over a fourth of Lee's service in the United States Army and therefore constitute a most important segment of his life and his military career.

However, before discussing his assignments west of the Father of Waters, I believe a summary of his life and career prior to 1837 is necessary background. Robert Edward Lee was born at Stratford, Westmoreland County, Virginia, on January 19, 1807. He was the fifth child of General Henry "Light Horse Harry" Lee and Henry's second wife Anne Hill Carter, the offspring of two of the best known and respected families in the Old Dominion State. Light Horse Harry Lee was one of Washington's favorite and most trusted cavalry officers. He had performed brilliantly during the Revolutionary War, fighting in both the Northern and Southern theaters of operation. Following our independence from Great Britain Henry Lee served as the Governor of Virginia and filled other positions of public trust before an ill conceived business venture and poor health forced him to leave the country. George Washington once wrote, "I know of no country that can produce a family all distinguished as clever men, as the Lees." His mother's family, the Carters, was just as distinguished.

Robert E. Lee's formal education prior to entering the United States Military Academy was extensive for that day. He first attended a private school administered by his mother's family, the Carters. At thirteen, he was enrolled in the Alexandria Academy to study under one of the finest teachers in Virginia, William B. Leary. Young Lee studied under Professor Leary for four years, and while waiting to secure his appointment to West Point, he enrolled for six months in Benjamin Hallowell's private school at Alexandria. Hallowell in later life was to write this about his famous pupil,

> He was a most exemplary pupil in every respect. He was never behind time in his studies, never failed in a single recitation; was perfectly observant of the rules and regulations of the institution; was gentlemanly, unobtrusive, and respectful in all his deportment to teachers and fellow students. He imparted a finish and a neatness, as he proceeded to do everything he undertook.

Hallowell's evaluation of Lee as a young man of seventeen could just as well have been said of him in the twilight of his life for all of these traits noticed by Hollowell appear time and again throughout his career, both military and civilian.

In 1825, at the age of eighteen, Robert E. Lee received the coveted appointment to West Point. Five senators and three representatives were among those who had endorsed his request for the appointment. The appointment was made by the South Carolina statesman, John C. Calhoun, who at the time was Secretary of War. It was Calhoun, incidentally, who had appointed Jefferson Davis to the Military Academy the year before (1824).

Lee graduated from West Point in 1829 with honors and without a demerit over a four year period. Only Douglas McArthur, graduating in 1903, would share this honor. Each year that Lee was at the academy, he was designated as a "Distinguished Cadet," an honor accorded to only the first five cadets in class standing. He was selected as the Adjutant of the Corps his senior year, a position awarded by the Superintendent to the cadet, who in his judgment, was the finest in the Corps. This was the prize of all academy achievements. Lee, during both his sophomore and his junior years was appointed staff sergeant and assistant professor of mathematics, teaching the plebes (freshmen), algebra and geometry. Robert E. Lee was graduated second in The Class of 1829 and was commissioned in the Corps of Engineers, the branch of the service reserved for the top graduates. The cadet who graduated first in The Class of 1829, Charles Mason, resigned two years after leaving the Academy, and his name has been lost to history.

Lieutenant Lee was assigned to several engineering projects prior to his St. Louis assignment in 1837. His first duty assignment after graduating from West Point in 1829 was to help construct a fort on Cockspur Island near Savannah, Georgia. It was hard work in a God-forsaken area of the country and the newly commissioned officer in the Corps of Engineers reported that he had "to spend many days in mud and water up to his arm pits." After some miserable months on the Georgia project in the spring of 1831 Lee was assigned to Old Point Comfort near Hampton Roads, Virginia. This was a little closer to home and civilization and gave the young Virginian a chance to be with some of his classmates from the Academy. While stationed here, Lee worked on several fortifications in the area including Forts Monroe and Calhoun (later renamed Wool). It was while stationed at Hampton Roads that he married Mary Anne Randolph Custis and here his first child was born, George Washington Custis Lee.

★ ────────── SIMPSON SPEAKS ON HISTORY ────────── ★

In late 1834, Robert E. Lee, still a second lieutenant, was transferred to Washington, D.C. as assistant to the Chief of Engineers, General Charles I. Gratiot. Most young officers would have considered this a plum, but it was primarily a desk job and therefore of little interest to Lee. However, several things of interest did occur while he was assigned to Washington. On the *engineering side* the Lieutenant helped to settle the boundary dispute between the State of Ohio and the Territory of Michigan by an extensive re-survey that took the entire summer of 1835. This dispute had threatened to erupt into a shooting war but Lee's work had prevented this. On the *career side*, he was promoted to First Lieutenant, and on the *family side*, two more children were born to the Lees while they were in Washington, Mary and William Henry Fitzhugh.

Lieutenant Lee's persistency to return to active field duty in the engineers finally paid off in the summer of 1837. General Gratiot, a native of Missouri, was very interested in the river that formed that state's eastern boundary, the Mississippi, and the state's largest city, St. Louis, and the serious problems that existed concerning the two. Engineer Lee would spend the next three years of his army service on the *St. Louis Project* and his first duty assignment "West of the River." It would be the first great engineering challenge of his life — a thirty year old army officer versus the two mightiest rivers in the United States — the Mississippi and the Missouri.

During this period of Lee's career two of his fellow officers left a physical description and character sketch of him. It is surprising how close the two evaluations are. Both of these officers were destined to play a major role in the Federal Army during the War Between the States. One was Lieutenant Montgomery C. Meigs, who had graduated from West Point with the Class of 1836 and had assisted Lee during his first year on the St. Louis project, and the other was Lieutenant Henry J. Hunt who was graduated from West Point in 1839 and was assigned to the Corps of Engineers. Meigs during the Civil War was Quarter-Master General of the Federal Army and Henry Hunt was Chief of Artillery for the Army of the Potomac. Meigs described Lee as being,

> . . . in the full vigor of youthful strength, with a noble and commanding presence, and an admirable, graceful and athletic figure. He was one with whom nobody ever wished or ventured to take a liberty, though kind and generous to all his subordinates, admired by all women, and respected by all men. He was the model of a soldier and the beau ideal of a Christian man.

Hunt saw Lee
> . . . as fine looking a man as one would wish to see, of perfect figure and strikingly handsome. Quiet and dignified in manner, of cheerful disposition,

always pleasant and considerate. He seemed to me the perfect kind of gentleman.

St. Louis, Missouri, founded in 1764, was a city of about 15,000 when Lee arrived there in 1837. It was the most important river terminal on the Upper Mississippi with some 300 steamboats using the port annually. It was the base of navigation for the river trade coming down the Mississippi, the Missouri, the Illinois and the Des Moines Rivers and it was the head of navigation for the larger boats from the Ohio and the Lower Mississippi. St. Louis was the "Gateway to the West" for wagon trains and travelers headed for California and Oregon and it was the focal point for a lucrative fur trade as well as for several other major industries from mining to milling. Seven states and two territories were vitally concerned with the future of St. Louis and no city in the United States of like population was so extensively engaged in trade. Remember, at this time there were no railroads to the West and the steamboat was the only rapid transportation of the day in that area.

St. Louis, however, had a serious problem, it was fast losing its status as a river port, and without a port there would be no city. The mighty Missouri, rolling downhill from the mountains and the uplands and the prairies 2400 miles away in the Northwest emptied into the Father of Waters a few miles above the city. The flow of the Missouri was so swift that it forced the slower flowing Mississippi to divert its main channel to the east or Illinois side of the river. As the dominant current of the Missouri swept into the Mississippi driving it toward the Illinois shore it left in its wake above St. Louis the great amounts of sand, mud and rock that it was carrying. This dropped debris caused a series of large mud and sand bars or islands to be formed above the city, fairly isolating it from the river. Real estate promoters and Eastern merchants, alarmed at having the harbor closed, shied away from investing in the city and when Lieutenant Lee reported for duty in the fall of 1837, St. Louis was in the midst of both an economic and an emotional depression.

Both the governor of the state and the mayor of the city had requested help from the Federal government. Technically, Washington could not aid the city as St. Louis had not been designated as a "port of entry." This oversight, however, was soon rectified when Congress designated the city as such a port in 1836, then immediately appropriated $15,000 "with which to build a pier to give directions to the current of the river Mississippi near St. Louis." Inasmuch as the amount was not deemed sufficient by the Corps of Engineers even to start, let alone finish the task, Congress the next year (1837) appropriated another $35,000. Once the funding was approved Robert E. Lee was assigned the formidable project, and a formidable project it was — changing the course of the Mississippi River.

Lee, leaving his wife and his three young children in Virginia, "in the care of five year old Custis Lee," he jokingly wrote, arrived in Missouri in the summer of 1837. After several weeks of work taming the rapids of the Des Moines River in northern Missouri, Lieutenant Lee reported for his work at St. Louis in August. His initial survey of the task and preliminary cost report showed the estimated cost to be almost $160,000. However, the $50,000 appropriated by Congress and another $15,000 appropriated by the City of St. Louis was all of the money allotted to the "Save St. Louis Project." Within two years time, using the relatively primitive equipment and tools of the day, and having but little manual help, Lee accomplished wonders. By building a series of dams, dikes, cuts, and channels he mastered the Mississippi.

Captain Lee (he was promoted while in Missouri) had harnessed the great river with his theory of dike and revetment-control and had returned the channel from the Illinois to the Missouri side. He had studied the dike system practiced in Holland, he had taken some ideas that had been used previously to control the Hudson River and by using his native engineering ability the young officer saved St. Louis as a river port. His major accomplishments on this project included removing an island of 200 acres covered with trees that had shut out the river for two miles in front of the city; building a three-quarter mile long dike from the Illinois shore to Bloody Island in the middle of the Mississippi to divert the current back to the Missouri shore; eliminating several large sand bars; pushing Duncan Island (the island blocking the port) a considerable distance downstream; and deepening the harbor from under six feet to over thirteen feet.

The young officer's method of river control engineering was adopted for use on most of the major rivers flowing into the Mississippi Basin. After the project was completed and he was re-assigned he continued to send advice and to answer questions for Henry S. Kayser, a German engineer whom he had trained as one of his assistants and who later became the City Engineer. Lee had so much confidence in this outpost on the Mississippi that he invested in both St. Louis municipal and Missouri state bonds anticipating a wave of prosperity after the river had been controlled. He was not to be disappointed. During the ten years following Lee's engineering feat the city progressed rapidly, it more than doubled in population

LEE WEST OF THE RIVER

and the number of steamboats using the river port almost tripled. Good times had returned once again to the port of entry on the Upper Mississippi.

St. Louis Mayor, John F. Darby, was much impressed with the young engineering officer. Soon after the project was completed he wrote,

> By his rich gift of genius and scientific knowledge Lieutenant Lee brought the Father of Waters under control . . . . I had made known to Robert E. Lee, in appropriate terms, the great obligation the authorities and citizens generally were under to him for his skill and labor in preserving the harbor . . . . One of the most gifted and cultivated minds I had ever met with, he was scrupulously conscientious and faithful in the discharge of his duties as he was modest and unpretending. He had none of that coddling and petty, puerile planning and scheming which men of little minds and small intellectual calibre use to make and take care of their fame. The labors of Robert E. Lee can speak for themselves.
>
> His time was occupied by making surveys, preparing drawings, and planning the manner of doing the work in the driving of piles and filling in with brush and stone, and in making revetments. I saw him almost daily; he worked most indefatigably, in that quiet, unobtrusive manner, and with the modesty characteristic of the man. He went in person with the hands every morning about sunrise, and worked day by day in the hot, broiling sun, the heat being greatly increased by the reflection from the river. He shared in the hard tasks and common fare and rations furnished to the common laborers — eating at the same table in the cabin of the steamboat used in the prosecution of the work, but never on any occasion becoming too familiar with the men. He maintained and preserved under all circumstances his dignity and gentlemanly bearing, winning and commanding the esteem, regard and respect of every one under him. He also slept in the cabin of the steamboat, moored to the bank near their work. In the same place, Lieut. Lee, with his assistant, Henry Kayser, worked at his drawings, plans and estimates every night till eleven o'clock.

Lee completed his work on the Mississippi in the fall of 1840, he had spent the thirty-first to the thirty-fourth years of his life on the project. It was his first independent assignment as a responsible supervising engineer and in these three years Lee progressed from being a promising young officer to an engineer of considerable skill with a recognized reputation in the Corps.

St. Louis a few years ago built a huge "golden" arch near the river front as a reminder of its nineteenth century status as the Gateway to the West. Instead of building this MacDonald type monument, however, what the City Fathers should have done is to have built a monument to Robert E. Lee on the river front, for without him there would be no city of St. Louis as we know it today.

Following the St. Louis assignment and prior to his second tour of duty west of the River during the Mexican War, Captain Lee's primary assignment was inspecting, repairing and modifying the cluster of fortifications in and around New York Harbor. It was during this time that he met and became acquainted with the Commanding General of the Army, Winfield Scott. The old veteran took a liking to Lee, and it proved to be a valuable acquaintance for the young officer.

Robert E. Lee's second assignment in the Trans-Mississippi area was prompted by his service in the Mexican War. This included a short stay in Texas (actually encompassing two short periods of time) followed by service in the field in Mexico. He had been graduated from West Point seventeen years before his first opportunity for field duty arrived. The opportunity came when the United States declared war against Mexico on May 31, 1846. Captain Lee left his engineering assignment at New York Harbor in late August, 1846, and was ordered to join General John W. Wool's Army then forming at San Antonio, Texas. After a short visit at Arlington, Lee traveled by steamer to New Orleans and then on to Port La Vaca, Texas, arriving in the Lone Star State on September 13. From here he rode to San Antonio arriving there on September 21.

General John E. Wool to whom Lee reported had assembled a 3,400 man army comprised of both regulars and volunteers, called the "Army of the Center." Wool, whose chief claim to fame prior to the Mexican War (and he gained little fame in that conflict) was that he had directed the removal of the Cherokee Indians from Georgia to the Indian Territory (Oklahoma) during Andrew Jackson's Indian removal program in the 1830's. With Wool's Army Lee shared engineering duties with Captain William D. Fraser, who had graduated from West Point first in the Class of 1834. Fraser had preceeded Lee to San Antonio and had made many of the engineering arrangements for the march of the army into Mexico before the Virginian arrived. Lee's principal duty, after he reported, was to collect supplies and tools for use in road building and bridging streams, two of the primary concerns for the engineers with an army that would be marching through the wastelands and the unbridged rivers of Northern Mexico.

The strategic plan for the American Army was a tri-pincers movement designed to take over all Northern Mexico and force a quick end to the War. Wool's Army was to march from San Antonio, Texas to Chihuahua City in North Central Mexico. General Zachary Taylor's Army at Fort Brown was to advance across the Rio Grande to Monterrey in Northeastern Mexico and a column of dragoons under General Stephen Kearny was to march from Ft. Leavenworth to Southern California by the way of Santa Fe. Kearny's objective was to take California and all intervening territory in the northwestern part of Mexico.

On September 28 the advance column of Wool's Army, 2,000 men, left the Mission City marching Southwest toward the Rio Grande. The rear column would follow in a few days with the supplies that arrived late. Lee rode with the advance column and although he was almost forty years old this was the first time that he had ever ridden with troops on a march against the enemy.

The advance into Mexico was to be uneventful. The 164 miles from San Antonio to the Rio Grande were accomplished in eleven days by 3,000 men, 2,000 horses and 1,100 wagons without a mishap, thanks to the road and bridge building supervised by engineers Fraser and Lee. The rapidity and the safety of the march was attributed by one observer, Frances Bayles, to "the indefatigable exertions of those distinguished officers, Captains Lee and Frazier (sic.) who built a road and bridged the streams." Upon reaching the Rio Grande Wool found the river high and the fords too deep and the current too swift to cross. Thus he was forced to camp on the north bank of the river while the engineers bridged it with pontoons. On October 12, the bridge was completed and the army crossed over into Mexico. Thus Lee's first tenure in Texas was short, one month.

When Wool reached Monclova, Mexico he learned that his objective had been changed and he was ordered to march east by the way of Parras toward Taylor's Army near Saltillo. Again Fraser and Lee, operating in advance of the army, supervised the building of roads and the bridging of streams. Their engineering ability enabled the marching column of men, horses, wagons and artillery to keep a steady pace, traveling at one time over 100 miles in four days. When Wool's Army reached Parras in December, 1846, it had traveled 365 miles into enemy territory without seeing a Mexican soldier and without a mishap.

The Army of the Center reached Saltillo in late December and here Wool joined forces with a large segment of Taylor's Army under General William J. Worth. Worth had been Commandant of Cadets at West Point when Lee was a cadet and according to Freeman, "to General Worth more than to anyone else Lee owed the military bearing that was to distinguish him throughout his military career." The 6,000 soldiers gathered at Saltillo were the largest body of troops that the Virginian had ever seen.

Campaigning without a shot fired in anger was about to end for Captain Lee. In mid-January, 1847, he received orders to join General Winfield Scott's Army forming at Brazos Santiago near Fort Brown, Texas, for a campaign against Mexico City. However, before leaving Saltillo, Engineer Lee assisted the army commanders in selecting a position of strength near the village of Buena Vista. This village would be the scene of one of the bloodiest battles of the war in late February. And although Lee would not be present at the battle of Buena Vista, the defensive position that he selected would play a major part in the great American victory there.

Lee left for Scott's Army on January 17, 1847, a few days before his fortieth birthday. Mounted on his mare *Creole* he rode the 250 miles through enemy country to Brazos Santiago, Texas, without incident. The assignment to Scott's Headquarters, Freeman wrote, "started Lee up the ladder of fame," and that it did. His outstanding performance during the Mexico City Campaign made an indelible impression on Scott, as subsequent events would bear out. A few weeks after Lee's arrival on the Texas coast, Scott's Army embarked for Mexican waters. With his West Point friend, Joseph E. Johnston as his cabinmate, Lee sailed from Texas on February 15 aboard the *Massachusetts*, Scott's command ship. The convoy stopped at Tampico on the East Coast of Mexico and then sailed south to Vera Cruz where the drive to Mexico City was to commence.

The American Expeditionary Force reached its destination — Vera Cruz on March 5, 1847. On the following day, as a member of a seaborne reconnaissance party, Lee came under hostile fire for the first time in his life, a wild cannonade from the castle fort guarding the Vera Cruz harbor. The bulk of Scott's Army landed safely at The Mexican Port on March 9. This was the first major amphibious landing made by an American army, a military manuever that would be perfected by the United States Army and Marines during World War II.

Captain Lee's record during the Mexico City campaign was nothing less than brilliant. He played a major engineering role in the reduction of the fort at Vera Cruz and his aggressive reconnaissance forays permitted Scott to outflank Santa Anna at Cerro Gordo and drive him back down the National Road toward the Mexican capital. Lee played a dominant part in both of the American victories at Contreras and Churubusco. Not only did he demonstrate his engineering skills but he conducted an active reconnaissance of Santa Anna's positions that dictated the thrust of Scott's attack. Prior to the above mentioned two battles, Lee while scouting the Mexican

Army had to cross three times, at night and in a rainstrom, a wild area of underbrush and uneven lava called the Pedregal. It was a physical feat of great effort that illustrated the engineer's bulldog tenacity and thorough dedication to duty.

The final battle of the campaign was the storming of the citadel of Chapultepec guarding Mexico City. Lee was particularly occupied with the construction of batteries and the placing of the guns for the bombardment of the Mexican Capital stronghold. Too, he conducted numerous scouting assignments close to enemy lines and was so actively employed that he went without sleep at one time for a forty-eight hour period. After the fall of the Mexican capital in early September, 1847, and until the peace treaty was concluded in the spring 1848, Lee and the other engineers were employed making surveys and preparing maps of Mexico City and vicinity. The maps were primarily concerned with the nearby battlefields of Contreras, Churubusco, Molino del Rey and Chapultepec. Captain Lee left Mexico City in late May, 1848 riding *Grace Darling*, his warhorse during the campaign. After arriving at New Orleans he took a steamer up to Wheeling, Virginia (now West Virginia) then by train to Washington, arriving home on June 29, 1848. He had been away for almost two years. Now he was home with his beloved family, his favorite dog Spec and his Maltese cats on whom he lavished much attention.

Twice during the Mexican war Lee narrowly escaped death. The first instance occurred was when he was returning from an inspection trip of the siege lines around Vera Cruz. Accompanied by Lt. P. G. T. Beauregard, Lee was making his way back to friendly lines at dusk when challenged by an American sentry. Although correctly answering the sentry's challenge, the nervous soldier fired point blank at Lee, the ball going between his arm and his body, so close that it singed his uniform. The second instance occurred during one of his reconnaissance trips prior to the battle of Cerro Gordo. Lee while in the rear of Santa Anna's front line was trapped at a spring from which the Mexican soldiers obtained their water. The Virginian had stopped at the spring to drink early in the morning. Before he could leave the area a large group of Mexican soldiers approached the spring to drink. Lee hid all day behind a large log near the spring as one group of soldiers after another came to fill their canteens. At times the soldiers were only a few feet away from the hidden American officer. Enduring the heat, insect bites and thirst until nightfall Lee made his way safely back to the American lines. He was slightly wounded at Chapultepec, the only wound that he would suffer during his military career.

Captain Robert E. Lee was brevetted three times during the Mexican War for "gallant and meritorious conduct." He received his first brevet to Major at Cerro Gordo, another to Lieutenant-Colonel at Churubusco and finally a brevet to Colonel at Chapultepec. The officers under whom Lee served during the various engagements were profuse with their praise for him. After Cerro Gordo, Colonel Bennett Riley wrote, "I cannot refrain from bearing testimony to the intrepid coolness and gallantry exhibited by Captain Lee . . . when conducting the advance of my brigade under the heavy flank fire of the enemy." But it was reserved for the commander of the Army to give Lee the highest plaudits for Cerro Gordo. "I am impelled to make special mention of the service of Captain R. E. Lee," Scott wrote. "This officer," he continued, "greatly distinguished at the siege of Vera Cruz, was again indefatigable during these operations, in reconnaissance as daring as laborious, and of the utmost value." Scott closed his report by saying, "Nor was he less conspicuous in planting batteries, and in conducting columns of these stations under the heavy fire of the enemy."

General David E. Twiggs in his report of the battle of Contreras and Churubusco mentioned Lee favorably. "To Captain Lee of the engineers," wrote Twiggs, "I have again the pleasure of tendering my thanks for the exceeding valuable services rendered throughout the whole of these operations . . . ." Generals Persifor Smith, Gideon Pillow and James Shields all commended Lee for his "skill and judgment." Scott's report of Lee's efforts at Contreras and Churubusco was as glowing as it had been for Cerro Gordo. In considering Lee's crossing of the Pedregal in the dark and in the rain, Scott was to remark that it was the "greatest feat of physical and moral courage performed by any individual in his knowledge ."

The military experience that the Virginian gained in Mexico would be of great benefit to him in the War Between the States. He particularly added to his text book knowledge of tactics and strategy. But, too, he learned from General Scott, the most experienced officer in the United States Army at the time, staff organization and operational planning and the value of communications and logistical support. Lee idolized the General and Scott thought very highly of his engineering officer. Several years after the War with Mexico Scott was to mention Lee in an official dispatch as "the very best soldier that I ever saw in the field."

LEE WEST OF THE RIVER

In the thirteen years between the Mexican War and the Civil War Robert E. Lee had three major assignments: chief engineer for the building of Fort Carroll in Baltimore Harbor; superintendent of the United States Military Academy at West Point; and duty in Texas with the Second United States Cavalry Regiment. It is the last of these assignments with which we are concerned and it would be Lee's third and last duty West of the Mississippi River.

On March 4, 1855 President Franklin Pierce signed a bill authorizing four new regiments in the United States Army, two cavalry and two infantry. This was the first time that two mounted regiments had been authorized by the Federal Government during peace time. The two mounted regiments were numbered the First and Second Cavalry and the two foot regiments were designated as the Ninth and Tenth Infantry. The Second Cavalry was organized specifically to serve on the Texas Frontier. Colonel Albert Sidney Johnston was the commander of the Regiment and Lt. Col. Robert E. Lee was designated second in command. This was a promotion for both officers. Administrative headquarters for the Second Cavalry was established at Louisville, Kentucky and the field headquarters (for logistics and training) was established at Jefferson Barracks, St. Louis, Missouri. While Johnston remained at Louisville he sent Lee to Jefferson Barracks to supervise the organizing, the supplying, and the training of the regiment. So after a lapse of some 15 years Robert E. Lee returned to Missouri.

The Virginian arrived at St. Louis in early June, 1855 and spent the summer shaping up the new command. He was no doubt very pleased to see the progress that the city had made since he had helped to restore it as a river port. In late September Lieut.-Colonel Lee was assigned to serve on a general court-martial at Fort Leavenworth, Kansas and did not ride with the regiment to Texas when it left Jefferson Barracks on October 27, 1855. Lee appeared to be a magnet for court-martial duty; following the court-martial at Fort Leavenworth he was assigned to the same duty at Fort Riley (Kansas Territory), then Carlisle Barracks (Penn.) and finally at West Point. In fact he did not re-join his regiment in Texas until March 11, 1856.

When Lee arrived in Texas in early March, he reported to Colonel Johnston at Regimental Headquarters at Fort Mason. Some two weeks later, after acquainting himself with the frontier situation, he was assigned to take command of the four companies at Camp Cooper in North Texas near the Comanche Indian Reservation. Lee arrived at Camp Cooper on April 7, and relieved Major William J.

Hardee who had been ordered to duty at West Point. Lee would remain in command here for over a year. However, much of his time would be taken up not in commanding Camp Cooper but in traveling through Texas on court-martial duty. From September, 1856 to July, 1857, he would be assigned to court-martial duty at the following widely separated locations: Ringgold Barracks, 700 miles south of Camp Cooper on the Rio Grande; Fort Brown near the mouth of the Rio Grande; Indianola on the Gulf Coast; and Fort Mason in West Central Texas. Fortunately, one trial during the period was held at Camp Cooper. Attending these military trials necessitated long rides, many through hostile country in regard to both inhabitants and climate and encompassing weeks of time. Lee reported that it was 112° in the shade when court was held at Camp Cooper, and that was the northern most location of the Court-Martial sites.

It did not take the commander of Camp Cooper long to become involved in the "search and seizure" policy that the War Department had recently put into effect for the Texas Frontier. This was an aggressive scouting or reconnaissance program designed to beat the Comanche and Kiowas at their own game. It was designed to intercept and then destroy their raiding parties before they could reach the frontier settlements or pass into Mexico. In early June, 1856 Lee commanded an expedition of four companies drawn from Camp Cooper and Fort Mason to ride west in an attempt to intercept Indian raiders that appeared to be headed for the Rio Grande. The four companies plus supply wagons and guides left on June 18 from their rendezvous point at Fort Chadbourne and rode west toward the headwater of the Brazos and Colorado rivers. The Lee expedition into Comanche country lasted 40 days, covered some 1,600 miles, and traversed thirty-two present Texas counties but netted little-two dead Indians, some property destroyed and 13 mules and horses captured. It was a gruelling campaign for both men and animals. Concerning the expedition, Lee was to write, "The weather was intensely hot, and as we had no tents we had the full benefit of the sun . . . the water was scarce and bad, salt, bitter and brackish." Although he would order several more expeditions into Comanche country while he was at Camp Cooper this was the only one that he led or participated in. Four years later, as Department Commander, he would take the field again but this time against Juan Cortinas along the Lower Rio Grande.

Lee remained at Camp Cooper for the rest of 1856, and into the summer of 1857, except for the General Courts-Martial Boards to which he was assigned. In July, 1857, Colonel Johnston was ordered to Washington and given command of the Utah Expedition organized to chastise Brigham Young and his Mormons. Lee succeeded Johnston in command of the Second Cavalry with Headquarters at San Antonio on July 28, 1857; however, his tenure of command of the elite regiment would be short, less than three months. On October 21, he received word that his father-in-law, G. W. P. Custis, had died at Arlington. Lee was granted a two months leave to go to Virginia to be with his wife, now a semi-invalid, and to administer the Custis estate. The Virginian left San Antonio on October 24 for Arlington and would not return to Texas again until mid-February, 1860. The Custis estate was complicated and difficult to settle, other problems arose while Lee was at Arlington including his involvement in the John Brown Affair, all of which necessitated that he be gone from his command for over two years.

When Lee arrived back in San Antonio on February 9, 1860, he found that he was in command of the Department of Texas; General Twiggs, the Department Commander, was on extended sick leave back in Georgia. As the commander of the Department, Lt.-Col. Lee was faced with a multitude of problems, the most serious being increased Comanche and Kiowa raids on the Northern and Western frontiers and the so-called ongoing Cortinas War along the Rio Grande. Although Juan Cortinas, the self-styled, "Robin Hood of the Rio Grande," had suffered a major defeat by a mixed force of soldiers and Texas Rangers a few months before Lee's arrival, he was still a force to contend with and drew the new department commander's attention as soon as he had taken command.

Lee took the field in person against the Mexican bandit in an effort to put an end to the turmoil along the Lower Rio Grande. He left San Antonio with a small escort on March 15, 1860 for Edinburg riding by the way of Eagle Pass. At Eagle Pass he was joined by two companies of the Second Cavalry and together the command continued south along the Rio Grande through Laredo and Ringgold Barracks to Edinburg, where he arrived on April 7. While they were near Laredo, a severe sleet storm struck the party freezing two men to death. On the trip from San Antonio to Edinburg, Lee, the engineer, maintained a strict schedule of march: reveille at 4 a.m., start the day's march at 5:30 a.m., and a final halt at 2 p.m. to make camp and graze their horses before dark.

When the Department Commander arrived at Edinburg he found the community in a state of great excitement. Just prior to his arrival, Mexican forces and Texas Rangers had exchanged shots across the river at Reynosa, just across the Rio Grande from Edinburg. Lee sent Captain Albert G. Brackett across the river with a flag of truce to determine the strength and the disposition of the Mexicans and to inquire about Cortinas. Brackett reported that Reynosa was fortified and ready for a fight, and that there were four companies of Mexican infantry in town plus a battery of artillery, but no Cortinas. However, the *Alcalde* (mayor) assured Brackett that Cortinas had left, that there would be no more firing, and that if the bandit did appear again he would be turned over to United States authorities. Thus an ugly situation was avoided. If required, Lee would have assaulted the town, and, if required, he would have ridden into the interior of Mexico in pursuit of Cortinas, whom the Mexican Government was accused of assisting. The Department Commander had specific orders from Secretary of War John Floyd "to stop Mexican depredations, and, *if necessary*, pursue the Mexicans beyond the limits of the United States." Lee, an aggressive commander, as was to be seen again and again during the Civil War, would not have hesitated to carry out the Secretary's orders, if circumstances had called for it. Lee returned to San Antonio in the early summer of 1860, but having little faith in the word of the Mexican officials left two companies of cavalry at Edinburg to guard the area.

While Colonel Lee and four companies of the Second Cavalry were concerned with the Mexican Robin Hood criss-crossing the Rio Grande, the other six companies of the regiment were busy repelling Comanche raids along the Northwestern frontier. The year 1860, when Lee was in command of the Department, was one of the busiest in Texas for the cavalrymen. They participated in seven engagements against the Red Marauders, several of them major affairs. As the year drew to a close General Twiggs returned from sick leave and again assumed command of the Department of Texas. Lee, after settling up his accounts and bidding his friends goodbye, on December 19, left San Antonio for Fort Mason, Headquarters for the Second Cavalry. He arrived at Fort Mason on Christmas Eve, and took command of the regiment on Christmas Day, 1860.

During this period of his career, while Lee was assigned to the Second Cavalry, he was described by a fellow officer as follows,

> He examined everything thoroughly and continuously, until the master of every detail, ever too conscientious to act under imperfect knowledge of any subject submitted to him and with all this stern sense of duty he attracted the love, the admiration and confidence of all. His sincerity, kindliness of nature and cordial manners attracting their unreserved confidence.

Another officer of the regiment wrote,

> He was one of the most agreeable men I ever knew. Handsome, courteous as a knight, pleasant and entertaining in conversation. He was universally beloved by all officers of his regiment.

There is little doubt that Robert E. Lee was one of the best liked and most respected senior officers in the United States Army.

The year 1861 opened with much foreboding concerning the continued existence of the Federal Union. South Carolina had already seceded and during the first month of the new year, the Old Palmetto State would be joined by the rest of the deep south — Mississippi, Florida, Alabama, Georgia and Louisiana in that order. Texas would secede the first day of February thus taking the last of the Gulf States out of the Union. General Twiggs' several enqueries to Washington on what to do with the Federal property and troops in Texas went unanswered. "The Bengal Tiger," one of Twiggs' better nicknames, was a Georgian and a secessionist, and failing to receive instructions from higher Headquarters took matters into his own hands. On February 18 he issued orders for all U. S. military posts in the Lone Star State to surrender to Texas State authorities. Thus Twiggs with one stroke of his pen, surrendered to Texas Secessionists, twenty-one Federal military posts, and ordnance, commissary and quartermaster supplies worth somewhere between 1.5 and 3 million dollars, and about $23,000 in cash. The amount in cash would have been greater had not Lieutenant Kenner Garrard, Company K, secreted $20,000 on his person when he left the State.

Lee had watched with some dismay the number of suspicious looking men lurking around Fort Mason since the first of the year and had received reports of like observations from the commanders of the other forts garrisoned by companies of his regiment. These groups of suspicious people (referred to by Texans as "Buffalo Hunters") grew more common causing the post commanders to make plans for defense and take steps to safeguard public property. Secession feelings ran high in Texas and all men dressed in Federal blue were looked on with suspicion. The Virginian was deeply concerned with the secession sentiments of the Texans and according to Captain Richard Johnson, who commanded the company that garrisoned Fort Mason, Colonel Lee called him in one day after Texas had left the Union (February 1) to discuss the defense of the fort with him. The Colonel proclaimed to Johnson in no uncertain terms that he was determined "to defend Fort Mason at all hazards" and asked Johnson, a Kentuckian, if he could rely on his support. After an affirmative answer "which seemed to please the Colonel very much," Johnson wrote, Lee "divulged to him his plan for fortifying the post." However, before he could put the plan into effect, Lee was transferred out of the Department.

Unfortunately, Lee's defense plan is not known, for neither he or Johnson put it in writing. However, considering the engineer that he was it was probably a very sound one. Lee we know was a Union man, a non-slave holder and against the process of secession. On numerous occasions in letters to his family and friends and in public statements, he made clear his stand on disunion. He also made clear, however, that his first loyalty was to his state — Virginia. Douglas Southall Freeman stated that Lee had little sympathy with the "Cotton State extremists" and that while "his mind was for the Union; his instinct was for the State of Virginia." As we all know now he was to follow his instinct.

In the midst of all of the sectional and national uncertainty the commander of the Second Cavalry, on February 4, received a message from General Twiggs ordering him to report to General Winfield Scott in Washington no later than April 1. Lee left Fort Mason on the morning of February 13 for San Antonio to begin his long trip to the East. As he was departing, Captain Johnson went to the ambulance in which Lee was riding and said to him, "Colonel, do you intend to go South or remain North? I am very anxious to know just what you propose to do." Lee replied, "I shall never bear arms against the United States — but it may be necessary for me to carry a musket in defense of my native state, Virginia, in which case, I shall not prove recreant to my duty." The driver cracked his whip, the ambulance was off and as it rolled away Lee thrust his head out of the window and shouted, "Good-bye, God bless you." This was the last time that Johnson saw his old commander and Fort Mason was Lee's last duty station in the Federal Army.

Lee reached San Antonio on February 16, the day that Ben McCulloch and his Texas Buffalo Hunters had seized the Federal installations and had taken over all Federal property in the city. He was appalled at what he saw and what had happened. The Texas State Troops attempted to arrest Lee and prevent him from leaving for Washington. After being detained several days and humiliated with what amounted to house arrest he was permitted to proceed to Indianola to board a ship for New Orleans. On February 22, (Washington's birthday) Lt. Col. Robert E. Lee, United States Army, left Texas for Virginia. The great soldier would not travel "West of the River" again.

THUNDER ON THE FRONTIER
THE 2ND U.S. CAVALRY IN TEXAS, 1855-1861

— COMPANY OF MILITARY HISTORIAN

UNIFORMS, 2nd U. S. CAVALRY, 1855-1861.
MUSICIAN, COMPANY OFFICER, PRIVATE (FATIGUES), CORPORAL FULL DRESS

The stable of Company G, Second U.S. Cavalry Regiment was alive with activity in the early morning hours of July 5, 1857. As the flickering lanterns sent their eerie yellow fingers of light along the stalls and among the rafters, twenty-four troopers of Company G, swearing and sweating, hurriedly saddled their brown mounts. Tim Shannon, First Sergeant of Company G, passed from man to man helping to adjust equipment, inspecting saddle bags — mess kit and personal belongings in one; hardtack, bacon and coffee in the other — and doling out ammunition, extra food and forage, enough for a month's campaigning.

With the call, "Boots and Saddles," each horse soldier who had finished checking weapons and adjusting equipment led out to the parade ground on the sloping crown of Post Hill. After the last cavalryman had left the picket stable, Sergeant Shannon, leading both his horse and Kentucky Belle, the lieutenant's favorite mount, made his way up the rocky slope, past the officers' quarters and joined his men on the quadrangle. The first light of dawn was streaking across the cloudless Texas sky as the sergeant formed his detail and awaited the appearance of the detachment commander.

The wait was short. From the direction of Regimental Headquarters, trailed by the famous Delaware Indian scout of the Second Cavalry John McLoughlin, strode the tall lean, tawny-bearded lieutenant, West Point graduate and man of action — John Bell Hood. With the grace of a born Kentucky horseman, Hood swung easily into the saddle, wheeled his big brown mare around, and faced his command. Crisp, clear orders rang out — "Stand to horse," "Prepare to mount," "Mount ho" and twenty-four horse soldiers slipped into their saddles and brought their skittish mounts into line.

Putting the troopers at ease, Hood briefed the tan, rugged group before him on the orders that he had received from Major George H. Thomas, acting regimental commander. The detachment, Lieutenant Hood said, was to ride west from Fort Mason along the North Llano to a point some fifteen miles the other side of Old Fort Terrett (Sutton County). The purpose of the expedition, he added, was to examine and explore an active north-south Indian trail that had been reported by Lieutenant John T. Shaaff, out on a scout a few days before. The Lieutenant asked for questions; receiving none, he brought the command to attention and then gave the orders: "Prepare to move out;" "Column of two's by the right flank, ho." To the squeaking of leather, the jingling of spurs, and the clanking of sabers, the column moved off the parade ground, through the garrison buildings, and down the eastern slope of Post Hill to the Fredericksburg Road and turned south toward the Llano. The early morning heat prophesied a hot, dusty march. The detachment of bantering troopers soon struck the river and turned west toward Comanche Country.

After the detail passed by the crumbling ruins of Fort Terrett, it turned northwest toward the Middle Concho and the desolate country beyond. Twelve days out, the scouting party discovered a fresh Indian trail that led toward the headwaters of the Devil's River and Mexico. Although the command was suffering greatly from thirst and the horses were exhausted, the Lieutenant did not hesitate to turn south and follow the trail. Hood and his men pressed on through the rugged wasteland; under a burning sun they barely survived on brackish water and reduced rations. Finally, after three days of hard riding, the horse soldiers caught up with their quarry — a mixed force of some one hundred Lipans and Comanches. The Indians, aware that they were being followed, stood at bay along a low range of hills east of Devil's river in far Southwest Texas.

On the afternoon of July 20, 1857, Company G of the Second U.S. Cavalry Regiment won its spurs on the Texas frontier. Outnumbered four to one, the troopers, their blue uniforms now gray from dust and soaked from sweat, closed with the half-naked, paint-smeared Comanches. Piles of brush fired by the squaws in an effort to confuse the horses and separate the soldiers blanketed the area in smoke. The fighting waged back and forth, with first one side and then the other gaining temporary advantage of the murky field. The Indians in an endeavor to stampede the soldier's mounts and unhorse the riders beat the horses about the head and neck with their buffalo hide shields. It was rifles, bows and arrows, lances and shields against carbines, six-shooters and sabers. Hood, although painfully wounded by an arrow that pinned his hand to the saddle, was everywhere encouraging his men on and providing aggressive leadership by example. The melee continuted unabated for some time; the fighting was primarily hand-to-hand and vicious with no quarter asked or given. As evening approached, the wailing of the squaws announced the withdrawal of the Lipans and Comanches from the field. The Indians, picking up their dead and wounded, disappeared through the Spanish bayonet and sagebrush toward the Rio Grande. The cavalrymen, too battered to follow, counted their casualties, cared for their wounded and moved to Devil's River where they bivouacked for the night. Hood reported seven casualties, two troopers killed and five wounded — three seriously. One cavalry mount was reported killed, three were wounded and all the horses were beaten badly about the head. The Indians had suffered heavily. Their losses, verified later by a Reservation Indian who had taken part in the engagement, numbered nineteen killed, including two minor chiefs, and probably as many wounded.

A relief column from the Eighth U.S. Infantry stationed at nearby Camp Hudson (Val Verde County), which had been summoned by Hood, arrived on July 21st with supplies and medical aid. The wounded of the Second Cavalry, with the exception of Hood, were left at Camp Hudson; the remainder of the detachment limped to Fort Clark (Kinney County) arriving there on July 27. Here the Lieutenant wrote the official report of the Devil's River Fight and forwarded it to San Antonio, headquarters for the Texas Military District. Hood's command, after remaining at Fort Clark for several days to rest the men and horses, rode back to Fort Mason, arriving there on August 8. The scouting detachment from Company G had been absent from its post for almost five weeks, had participated in a major Indian engagement, and had ridden over 500 miles through desolate country under extremely adverse conditions.

The Devil's River Fight was one of several major Indian engagements fought by the Second Cavalry while it was stationed in Texas. Hood's extensive reconnaissance mission from Fort Mason was a routine operation for the cavalrymen and was a good example of the regiment's aggressive attitude towards the red marauders. Too, the conduct of the officer and the men in the affair on July 20 was typical of the attitude, discipline, and morale of the personnel assigned to the famous mounted unit.

The Second U.S. Cavalry Regiment was authorized by an act of Congress passed in early March, 1855. Included in the same act was authorization for another mounted regiment, the First Cavalry, and two foot regiments, the Ninth and Tenth Infantry. Never before in the United States during peacetime conditions had two mounted regiments been authorized at the same time. "Such generousity (*sic*) by Congress," wrote one military historian, was "looked upon as almost a miracle; but the necessities of the country demanded it, and our lawmakers widely acquiesced." Three mounted regiments existed in the army at the time of the March, 1855 authorization — the First and Second Dragoons and the Mounted Rifles. The two Dragoon regiments had been authorized in 1833 and 1836, respectively, and the Mounted Rifles in 1846.

The Second Cavalry, often referred to as "Jeff Davis's Own," was an elite organization — perhaps the finest regiment to be organized in the American army. Jefferson Davis was accused of hand picking the officers for the Regiment, the greatest percentage of them being like himself, graduates of the United States Military Academy and Southerners by birth. Of the thirty-four officers who were initially assigned to the Regiment or who joined it at Jefferson Barracks prior to its march to Texas, twenty-four were from states below the Mason-Dixon Line, and twenty of these were West Point graduates. It has long been argued among military historians as to whether or not the Secretary of War purposely assigned to the Second Cavalry outstanding officers of Southern birth and trained at West Point. Those who support this theory contend that Davis saw the Civil War coming and visualized the officers of the Regiment being used as the nucleus for a future Southern Army. George H. Thomas, a Virginian, was one of the few Southern officers in the Regiment who did not resign his commission in 1861 and "Go South."

The non-commissioned officers for the Second Cavalry were especially selected from the other mounted regiments, and the privates were recruited from all sections of the nation. Company A was recruited from Alabama; Company B from Virginia; Company C from Pennsylvania; D Company from Maryland; Company E from Missouri; F Company from Kentucky; Company G, nation-wide; Company H from Indiana and Illinois; and K Company from Ohio.

Horses for the Regiment were purchased by a special team of Second Cavalry officers who were authorized to buy the best blooded stock available in Kentucky, Indiana and Ohio. This wise purchasing policy bore fruit. After constant use for six years on the Texas Frontier most of these horses were still serviceable. For purposes of appearance and to engender esprit-de-corps, each company was assigned horses of a single color, Company A had greys; Companies B and E, sorrels; Companies C, D, F & I were assigned bays; G & H Companies had brown horses; and Company K had roans. If a horse of one color became unserviceable, it was replaced by a horse of the same color in order to maintain the company's appearance.

In concert with the high standards set in selecting the men and mounts, the Regiment was furnished with the newest and best arms, accouterments and equipment. Five of the ten companies were issued new experimental shoulder arms — three were armed with Springfield rifle-carbines, one with the Springfield movable stock carbine and one with the breech loading Perry carbine. Each man in the Regiment was armed with a Colt Navy revolver and a dragoon saber. One company was provided with gutta-percha or leather scabbards and pistol holsters and gutta-percha cartridge boxes. All enlisted men were supplied with leather saber belts and carbine slings. Six companies were issued new Campbell saddles which were brass mounted and provided with wooden stirrups. A gutta-percha talma (rain coat) having loose sleeves and extending to the knees was issued to each man in the regiment.

The senior officers appointed to the Second Cavalry had outstanding records, and the captains and lieutenants were young men of great promise. In order to obtain the best officers possible, several proven leaders were selected from civilian life. Of the thirty-four officers first appointed to the Regiment, as noted previously, twenty were West Point graduates and fourteen were from civilian life. The highest ranking civilian appointees were Captains Theodore O'Hara, Charles Travis, Albert Brackett and William Bradfute; all had considerable Mexican War experience or extensive Indian fighting experience. Most of the remaining appointees from civilian life had nearly all had seen some frontier service against the Indians, The Texas Rangers were tapped for one man, Charles E. Travis, the only son of the Commander of the Alamo, Colonel William Barrett Travis. Unfortunately, young Travis was court-martialed under questionable circumstances and dismissed from the service before the Regiment reached Texas. Ben McCulloch of both Mexican War and Texas Ranger fame made it known that he would like to command the Second Cavalry, but was only offered the rank of major in the First Cavalry Regiment. Considering himself worthy of higher rank, McCulloch refused the commission.

Colonel Albert Sidney Johnston of Texas was appointed to command the Second Cavalry, and Lieutenant Colonel Robert E. Lee of Virginia was designated as second in command. William J. Hardee, a Georgian, was assigned as the senior major, and after Major William H. Emory transferred to the First Cavalry, Major George H. Thomas, another Virginian, was appointed the junior major. Earl Van Dorn of Mississippi was the senior captain of the Second and commanded Company A. Other captains and company commanders were E. Kirby Smith (Co. B), James Oakes (Co. C), Innis N. Palmer (Co. D), George Stoneman, Jr. (Co. E), Theodore O'Harra (Co. F), William R. Bradfute (Co. G), Charles E. Travis (Co. H), Albert G. Brackett (Co. I), and Charles J. Whiting (Co. K). Of the twenty Lieutenants in the regiment, Nathan G. "Shanks" Evans, West Point Class of 1848, ranked first and Robert C. Wood, Jr. who entered the Military Academy in 1854 but resigned to accept a second lieutenancy in the Second Cavalry, ranked last. Rupert Richardson, Southwest Frontier historian, succinctly expressed the opinion of military historians when he wrote, "the officers corps of the Regiment [2nd Cavalry] consisted of the greatest aggregation of fighting men that ever represented the United States Army in the Old West."

Although the headquarters for Johnston's Regiment was established at Louisville, Kentucky, in April 1855, the Regiment was actually formed during the summer and early fall of that year at Jefferson Barracks, Missouri. Here the companies were organized and trained and their officers assigned. Some difficulties were experienced at Jefferson Barracks during the organization period: cholera made a brief appearance, quartermaster stores were late in arriving and military restraints and daily drills caused some dissatisfaction and a number of desertions. In early September the Regimental Headquarters was transferred from Louisville to Jefferson Barracks, and in the latter part of the month orders were received transferring the Regiment to the Texas Frontier. However, it would be a month before the Second Cavalry left Jefferson Barracks.

The trek West commenced on the morning of October 27, 1855, and proceeded per orders "by easy marches across the country to Fort Belknap, Texas." It was an imposing sight, a sight that would have thrilled the likes of film directors John Ford, Raoul Walsh and Howard Hawks to see this splendid Regiment ride from Jefferson Barracks early on the morning of October 27, 1855. Trumpets sounded "Boots and Saddles," at 4 a.m. and at 6 a.m.; the long column, some 700 men, 750 horses, 29 wagons and 5 ambulances, commenced its march. After clearing the post, the column turned west and headed for Fort Belknap, the initial destination of the Regiment in Texas.

All company equipment and property, surplus baggage of the officers, and the company laundresses were sent to Texas by water via New Orleans and Indianola under the command of Lieutenant J. H. McArthur. Except for the usual disciplinary problems and foraging escapades the movement to Texas was uneventful — no hostile Indians, no epidemics and no serious losses of men, horses or wagons. Through Missouri in a southwesterly direction rode the horse soldiers. Over the Ozark Mountains, across the northwest corner of Arkansas, and into Indian Territory rode the long blue line. Through the reservations of the Cherokees, the Seminoles, the Creeks and the Choctaws, Johnston led his seemingly endless column of men, horses and wagons. On December 12, 1855, the Regiment arrived at Fort Washita (Indian Territory) and was given a resounding reception, a reception that included a thirty-gun salute by Captain Braxton Bragg's Battery.

The Second Cavalry crossed the Red River into Texas at Preston (Grayson County) on December 15. As the conveyance carrying the commander's family reached the south side of the river, Johnston's daughter Maggie shouted, "This is my country, hurrah for Texas." The Lone Star State, however, seemed anything but hospitable and certainly nothing worth shouting about to the men who had come to protect her frontiers. A blue norther swept down on the command the evening of December 22 when it was camped near Buffalo Springs (Clay County). The temperature dropped to four degrees below zero, water froze inside the tents, and meat was frozen so hard it could not be cut with an axe. The wind blew with hurricane force pelting the shivering soldiers and animals with hail, sleet and snow. On the following day the weather was so cold and miserable that "several horses were frozen to death on the picket lines," the women and children stayed in bed until noon, and the Regiment was unable to march. For the balance of December the thermometer remained "uniformly below zero," and on the day tht the cavalrymen rode into Fort Belknap (Young County), December 27, "113 oxen belonging to a wagon train encamped nearby were frozen to death." Within a few months the Regiment would witness the other uncomfortable extreme in Texas weather.

At Fort Belknap orders assigning the companies to their initial stations in Texas were waiting for Johnston. Headquarters and Companies B, C, D, G, H, and I under Colonel Johnston were directed to reoccupy Fort Mason (Mason County), a former Second Dragoon post abandoned two years previously. Major Hardee, the senior major of the regiment, was ordered to take companies A, E, F, and K and establish a new outpost on the Clear Fork of the Brazos near the Brazos Indian Reservation (Throckmorton County), some forty miles southwest of Fort Belknap. This post, which was established to watch the Northern and Middle Comanches, was named Camp Cooper in honor of the Adjutant-General of the Army, Samuel Cooper.

Colonel Johnston and the six companies assigned to Fort Mason left Fort Belknap on January 2, 1856. After negotiating the icy waters of the Clear Fork of the Brazos, the Pecan, the Colorado and the San Saba, they arrived at their destination on January 14. The abandoned outpost was in a bad state of repair. Local settlers had stripped many of the buildings of doors, windows and siding in what appeared to have been a systematic community effort of "moonlight requisitioning." Except for a few officers' quarters and storeroom buildings nothing else was habitable; consequently, a tent city sprang up near the springs north of the fort. The soldiers were soon put to work repairing the old buildings and raising new ones, and by late spring Fort Mason flourished again.

Major Hardee's command of four companies arrived at the Clear Fork of the Brazos on January 3 and established Camp Cooper "about one mile above the Indian village reservation." The men lived in tents during the hard winter and suffered severely but it was the horses that bore the brunt of the northers that followed each other in rapid succession. There was no material available to erect shelters for the animals, so they were picketed in the open and "were frequently covered with frozen sleet." Having been exposed to the frigid weather during the winter, many of the horses died from the staggers (congestion of the brain) when warm weather came. Regardless of the inclement weather and physical discomfort, the soldiers were encouraged to hunt in the vicinity of the camp. Such activity would not only provide recreation for the men and food for the camp, but according to one biographer of the command, would "assist in educating (the soldiers) to ride, shoot, and acquire a knowledge of the adjacent country." Under these unfavorable circumstances the companies at Camp Cooper spent the remainder of the winter.

The five years that the Regiment was stationed south of the Red River were years of action. The War Department had changed its strategy in regard to frontier warfare in Texas. As had been the case earlier in the decade, the mounted garrisons would no longer merely maintain a defensive patrol cordon and react only to Indian aggression. This defensive policy had hobbled the activities of both the Second Dragoons and Mounted Rifles who had patroled Texas earlier in the decade. With the posting of the Second Cavalry along the Frontier, the War Department advocated a policy of long range scouting to ferret out the Indians. Patrol, pursue and punish was the new strategic concept. Keep as many reconnaissance and scouting forces in the field as possible, find the Comanche, the Kiowa and the Apache trails, follow them relentlessly, and bring the marauders to battle; this was the policy advocated by the department commander. This procedure was followed religiously by the post commanders, and by 1861 the red raiders had been brought to battle dozens of times and their area of maneuverability greatly restricted.

On Washington's birthday, 1856, the Second Cavalry drew its first blood in Texas. Captain James Oakes with a detachment from Company C left Fort Mason on February 14, just two months after the regiment had entered the Lone Star State. Oakes was in pursuit of a band of Waco (Huaco) Indians, reported to have been lifting scalps and stealing horses southwest of the fort in what is now Kimble County. A frenzied settler had ridden in with the news. On the third day out, the detachment picked up the trail of the Indians and followed it for six days. Finally the cavalrymen caught up with the marauders and brought them to battle just west of old Fort Terrett on February 22. The Wacos were routed, several being killed or wounded. Two men of Company C were severely wounded, and arrows passed through the uniforms of several others. The soldiers were exposed to cold, wet weather, and they ran out of food on the way back to Fort Mason. Several of the beautiful bays of Company C had to be eaten.

The Regiment was involved in forty engagements, scores of patrols and scouting assignments, and numerous escort missions during its five year tenure in Texas. In some instances there were as many as three scouting details from a fort out on patrol at one time. All but three of the forty battle actions occurred within the borders of the Lone Star State. Twice, once in 1858 and again in 1859, dashing Earl Van Dorn penetrated deep into the Indian Territory and the Kansas Territory to engage hostile Comanches, and in 1860 Captain George Stoneman, Jr., led a raid against Cortinas and his men south of the Rio Grande. The greatest number of casualties suffered by the regiment was at Wichita Village (Indian Territory) on October 1, 1858, and at Small Creek (Kansas Territory) on May 12, 1859. In the former battle five cavalrymen were killed and ten wounded, and in the latter two were killed and thirteen wounded. Fortunately, in only two other engagements did the dead and wounded total as many as a half dozen. Hood, at Devil's River on July 20, 1856, suffered seven losses, and Major George H. Thomas in a battle with the Comanches on August 26, 1860, reported six casualties. Altogether, the Second Cavalry had thirteen men killed and fifty-eight wounded while guarding the Texas Frontier in the half decade prior to the Civil War.

The two most successful battles fought by the mounted regiment were Earl Van Dorn's two major expeditions against the Comanches north of the Red River. Captain Van Dorn, called by one military historian the "most dashing cavalry officer in Texas before the Civil War," left Fort Belknap in mid-September 1858, with a combined force of four cavalry companies and sixty friendly Indians. In order to surprise the hostile Comanches, the cavalrymen and their Indian allies rode the last ninety miles in thirty-eight hours. The men were in the saddle continuously for eighteen hours during one stretch of the forced ride. In a desperate two hour, hand-to-hand struggle on

October 1 near Wichita Village in the Choctaw Nation, the red marauders were badly beaten and scattered. Their encampment and supplies were destroyed, 300 of their ponies were captured, and between fifty and sixty of their warriors lay dead on the field. General David E. Twiggs, commander of the Texas Military District at the time, termed Van Dorn's achievement at Wichita Village, "A victory more decisive and complete than any recorded in the history of the Indian warfare."

The following year the irrepressible captain led a second expedition into the lair of the same hostile band. In late April 1859, at the head of a command composed of six companies of the Second Cavalry and fifty-eight Indian allies, Van Dorn moved north from Camp Radziminski (Indian territory) into Kansas territory. After a trek of 200 miles, a large Comanche village was sighted just north of old Fort Atkinson on Small Creek near the Nescutunga, a tributary of the Arkansas. Forewarned of Van Dorn's approach, the warriors had selected a strong defensive position in a brush covered ravine. In another hand-to-hand encounter, with no quarter asked or given, the Comanches were finally driven from their stronghold and scattered, losing fifty killed, five wounded and thirty-six taken prisoner. One hundred ponies as well as much equipment and many supplies were also taken.

Major-General J. K. Herr, the last Chief of Cavalry of the United States Army, wrote that "these two engagements [Wichita Village and Small Creek] were the most decisive victories gained to that time over those Ishmaels [Comanches] of the Southwest."

The last major engagement fought by the Regiment before leaving the Lone Star State occurred along the Pease River in mid-December, 1860. Here, First Sergeant John W. Spangler, leading a detachment from Company H and a detail of State Forces from Camp Cooper, engaged a large party of Comanches on December 19. After a spirited fight, Spangler's command killed fourteen warriors, wounded an undisclosed number and captured three "without loss or serious hurt to the victors." Thus was attached the last battle streamer to the regimental colors of the Second United States Cavalry Regiment during its assignment on the Texas Frontier.

As was the custom of the day, the officers led the men into battle, and consequently several officers were numbered among the killed and wounded. Second Lieutenant Cornelius Van Camp was killed instantly by an arrow through his heart while leading a charge at Wichita Villge on October 1, 1858. Major George H. Thomas, Captains Earl Van Dorn and E. Kirby Smith and Lieutenants John B.

Hood, Fitzhugh Lee, James B. Witherell and Robert C. Wood, Jr., were wounded, several of them seriously. Major Thomas, later to gain Civil War fame as the "Rock of Chickamauga," proved his granite constitution and construction prior to the fratricidal conflict. On August 26, 1860, in an engagement with the Comanches on the Salt Branch of the Brazos, the Major turned two arrows, one barbed shaft cutting and glancing off of his heavily bearded chin and a second one off of his hairy chest. Van Dorn was wounded the most number of times, four, and also was the most seriously wounded. The impulsive and spirited captain received a wound at Wichita Village that proved almost fatal. An arrow was shot through his body from side to side. It passed through his rib cage twice, cut his left lung and went through the upper part of his stomach. If this wound did not prove fatal, it is difficult to see why the trip back to the base camp did not kill the plucky Mississippian; it was an eighty mile ride over rough country in a crude litter fastened between two mules. Within two months, the indomitable captain was back in the saddle again in Texas. Van Dorn lived through this close brush with death only to be murdered in a love triangle during the Civil War.

While many of the officers of the Second Cavalry engaged in acts of bravery above and beyond the call of duty, I believe that Lieutenant Fitzhugh Lee of Company B, a nephew of Robert E. Lee, takes the cake in this category. In mid-January, 1860, a Comanche raiding party was reported to have stolen a large number of horses and mules from settlers close to Camp Cooper and was headed south with the herd. Lee, who had just returned from witnessing the inauguration of Governor Sam Houston at Austin, volunteered to lead a detail of twelve troopers in pursuit of the raiders. Soon after the men left Camp Cooper, they ran into a blue norther, but in spite of the blowing snow Lee picked up a faint trail and followed it south. After riding 18 hours without halting the cavalrymen finally stopped to camp. No fires were allowed and the men "feasted on hard tack and frozen pork." After three days on the trail the norther finally blew out making the raiders easier to follow. On the afternoon of January 17, the troopers caught up with the horse thieves driving the stolen herd up Pecan Bayou in present day Calahan County.

The Comanches wrapped in their blankets were unaware of Lee's approach and when the Lieutenant and his men charged they were caught by surprise. Too dumbfounded to make a stand, the Comanches broke for a nearby stand of timber except for the two warriors guarding the rear of the herd — they had no choice but to stand and fight. One of these was shot and killed by a trooper, and the other, in defiance to Lee, turned and fired two arrows at the Lieutenant and then fled. Lee was not about to be shot at, so he, his bugler, and a trooper took off after the galloping Comanche. The warrior led the cavalrymen on a cold seven mile chase in and out of the timber, finally the Indian abandoned his spent pony and ran into a rocky ravine with Lee and his two men in close pursuit. The Lieutenant and the bugler entered the ravine on foot, the trooper holding their horses. Lee was armed with an "old fashioned muzzle-loading carbine" and a Navy Colt revolver, and was wearing his heavy winter overcoat and cape. The heavy wearing apparel proved to be a life saver for the young officer.

The two cavalrymen searched the area carefully and as Lee approached a rocky ridge near the end of the ravine, the Comanche suddenly jumped out and shot an arrow at short range directly at him — the third arrow he had taken from the same warrior. Lee jumped aside and the arrow passed through the left sleeve of his coat and his cape, and shattered the stock of the carbine that he was carrying. The Indian was on him in a flash and as young Lee attempted to use his pistol, the warrior grasped the barrel and turned it aside as the gun fired. In the struggle for the pistol it dropped to the ground and then followed a "desperate hand-to-hand struggle," with the Comanche using his knife and the Lieutenant trying to avoid the thrusts and the slashings. Finally Lee, in a quick manuever embraced his opponent in a bear hug, placed his foot behind the Indian's heel and succeeded in throwing him backward to the ground with the burly Lieutenant on top. As luck would have it, the pistol was within the reach of Lee who freed his right arm, cocked the pistol and shot the warrior through both cheeks. A second shot, better aimed, killed the Comanche instantly. Few other officers in the Indian Fighting Army, if any, could claim to have killed an Indian warrior in a personal, one-on-one encounter.

Fortunately for the Lieutenant, he was not wounded, although his heavy coat was slashed in many places. Lee, when queried by his fellow officers on how he succeeded in throwing the Comanche replied,

> He, the Indian, was very strong as far as brute strength went, but he knew nothing of the science of wrestling. For a time though, I thought that he would get me, when I happened to think off a trick in wrestling which I had learned during my school days in Virginia. It was known as the "Virginia back heel." I tried it on him and *fotched* him down.

While Fitzhugh Lee himself was highly commended for his leadership and bravery in both Department and Army orders, he in turn, praised several of his men for their conduct in his report of the engagement.

Leadership by example was a mark of the officers of the Second Cavalry; Hood at Devil's River in 1857, Van Dorn at Wichita Village in 1858 and now, Fitzhugh Lee at Pecan Bayou in 1860, were just a few of the examples.

One of the strengths of the elite Cavalry Regiment was the high caliber of its non-commissioned officers — the backbone of any military unit and the unsung heroes of the Indian Fighting Army. Fittingly, a sergeant led the last contingent of the Second Cavalry to see action in Texas and many of the Regiment's most successful encounters were led by two and three stripers. Of the forty encounters in Texas, non-commissioned officers led the Federal forces into battle ten times, and many of the casualties of the Second Cavalry wore stripes on their sleeves. Three non-commissioned officers (all sergeants) were killed in action and eight were wounded. Several sergeants and corporals were cited in official orders for "conspicuous gallantry and unflinching courage." First Sergeants Walter McDonald (Company D) and John W. Spangler (Company H) were specifically cited for such conduct on two occasions. Spangler was later commissioned a second lieutenant in the Third U. S. Cavalry during the Civil War and at Gettysburg recieved a brevet captaincy "for gallantry and meritorious service."

Not only were the officers and the non-commissioned officers of superior caliber, but apparently the select recruiting for the Regiment conducted throughout the United States in 1855 paid dividends. Time and again the gallant conduct of private soldiers in action was cited in General Orders and commanders' battle reports. One company commander in particular was profuse in his praise of the enlisted men that composed his unit. Captain R. W. Johnson of Company F wrote that he did "not believe that a more superior lot of men could have been found in the army" than those constituting his company. "About forty of them," he said, "weighed from one hundred and forty to one hundred and fifty pounds . . . . Each was an excellent horseman, afraid of nothing, never tired, and always cheerful, and always willing to endure fatigue and hardship, if I exacted it of them." No doubt the other captains, had they written their memoirs, would have verified Johnson's observation in relations to their own companies.

In order to effectively guard the outlying settlements, the companies of the Regiment were scattered along the perimeter of the frontier from the Red River on the north to Fort McIntosh on the Rio

Grande. As noted previously, when the Second Cavalry was first assigned in Texas its companies occupied only two frontier posts. Colonel Johnston and six companies were stationed at Fort Mason, while Major Hardee and the other four companies established Camp Cooper. The companies remained at these two posts during the first few months they were in Texas. When the Mounted Rifles were withdrawn from the state in the summer of 1856, the Second Cavalry was the only mounted unit left in Texas. Only once during the remaining four and one-half years was the burden of guarding 2,000 miles of border and frontier shared with another mounted unit. Sometime during 1859, five companies of the First Cavalry were assigned to the Department of Texas, but apparently they were soon transferred out of the State. There is no record of units of the First Cavalry engaging Indians in Texas prior to the Civil War.

After the withdrawal of the Mounted Rifles in July, 1856, the companies of Johnston's command were widely distributed along the frontier to afford maximum protection to the State. Companies A and F were posted to Camp Colorado (Coleman County); Companies B and G, along with the regimental headquarters and band, remained at Fort Mason; Company C was assigned to Fort Clark (Kinney County); Company D was ordered to Camp Verde (Kerr County); Company K was sent to Fort Inge (Uvalde County); and Company I was assigned to Camp Sabina (Uvalde County). While the Regiment remained in Texas, company reassignments between frontier posts would be frequent. The rapidly changing Indian situation and the gradual westward movement of the frontier dictated the establishment of new posts and the abandonment of old ones. At one time or another, either on a temporary or on a permanent basis, companies of the Regiment occupied nineteen established camps and forts in Texas. Only in one instance was an established campsite out of Texas occupied for any length of time by a unit or units of the Regiment. From September 1858 to September of the following year, Companies A, B, C, F, G and H, at the same time and at different times, were stationed at Camp Radziminski located on Otter Creek in the Indian Territory. Camp Radziminski was abandoned permanently in September 1859.

The Second Cavalry was commanded at one time or another by Johnston, Lee, Thomas and Van Dorn during its deployment to Texas. Albert Sidney Johnston commanded the famed unit until July 29, 1857 when he was ordered to Washington and given command of the Utah Expedition against the Mormons. Robert E. Lee succeeded Johnston as commander, but within three months he was granted an extended leave of absence to Virginia, and was replaced by Major George H. Thomas. When Thomas was granted a year's leave of absence on November 12, 1860, he was replaced by Captain Earl Van Dorn. Lee again assumed command of the regiment on December 24, 1860, and retained command until he was ordered to Washington by General Scott in mid-February, 1861. The great Virginian was the last official commander of the Second Cavalry while it was stationed in the Lone Star State and it was the last command that he held in the United States Army.

In a special convention Texas voted to secede from the Union on February 1, 1861. General David Emanuel Twiggs, commander of the Department of Texas, was induced without too much persuasion to surrender all of the Federal military installations in Texas to State Confederate authorities. Thus was perpetrated one of the biggest giveaway programs in American military history. Twenty-one military installations, between 1.5 and 3 million dollars worth of military stores and supplies and $23,472 in cash were seized by state military forces. Too, some 2,500 troops, fifteen per cent of the Regular Army at the time, were put out of action.

If Lee had not been called to Washington in February of 1861 but had remained at Fort Mason in command of the Second Cavalry, would he have surrendered his command to Texas State authorities? There is some reason to believe that Lee might have resisted the takeover of Federal property by the Texas "Buffalo Hunters." According to Captain Johnson, Colonel Lee had discussed with him one day in early February 1861 the defense of Fort Mason, remarking to Johnson that "he was determined to defend Fort Mason at all hazards." Lee was not a secessionist and was not in favor of the movement. He was a Union man and a non-slaveholder. It was only when he returned to Virginia and saw how his native state felt about secession that he embraced the cause. Had the great Virginian remained in Texas another month or so, the Civil War could very well have started in the Lone Star State instead of in South Carolina. After all, some 700 well mounted, well-led and well-equipped cavalrymen would have been a force to be reckoned with by Texas authorities.

The commanderless Second Cavalry, as did the other Federal units in the state, complied with Twigg's "Order of Exercise" or surrender order and made arrangements to abandon their stations. The exodus of the cavalry from Texas began in late February 1861, continued through March and was completed in early April. Even as the surrender order was being promulgated, the Regiment continued to discharge its duty as protector of the frontier. In mid-February, Lieutenant A. K. Arnold with a detachment from Company C left Fort Inge in pursuit of a band of hostile Comanches reported to have been raiding settlements in present day Kinney County. Arnold pursued the Indians so closely that they were forced to take refuge in Mexico. "Thus," wrote the somewhat bitter biographer of the Regiment, "to the very last hour the Regiment discharged its duty to the State, even when the citizens had renounced the flag of their country . . . ." Arnold's pursuit was the last recorded action by the Second Cavalry in Texas.

The mounted companies, per instructions, were ordered to march from their far flung stations and rendezvous at Green Lake in western Calhoun County. From here they were to march to Indianola where they were to embark on ships for Northern assignments. Companies B, D, H, and I, which were stationed nearest to the coast arrived at the rendezvous point first. They were soon joined by Companies E and G, which had been transported by water down the Rio Grande and through the Gulf to Indianola, and then had marched overland to Green Lake. These six companies constituted the first detachment of the Second Cavalry to leave the State. Under the command of Captain I. W. Palmer, the companies marched to Indianola and on March 31 embarked on the steamship *Coatzacoalcos* for New York where they arrived on April 11, 1861. The second detachment, composed of the Regimental Headquarters and Companies A, C, F and K, gathered at Green Lake a few days after the first group, marched to Indianola, boarded the steamer *Empire City,* and arrived in New York on April 20. Thus was completed the movement of the Second U. S. Cavalry from Texas.

The regiment left behind it a proud military heritage. The mounted companies had driven the Indians far beyond the fringes of settlement and had attacked the hostile Comanches deep in their heartland. Audacious in reconnaissance, determined in pursuit and successful in battle, the Second Cavalry made a significant contribution to Texas Frontier history.

After the return of the Second Cavalry to New York, it was assigned to Carlisle Barracks, Pennsylvania, for re-equipping and re-organization. During the spring and summer of 1861, the companies of the Regiment were assigned to various Federal army units in the East. Several of the companies saw action in the early engagements of the Civil War. An act passed by Congress on August 3, 1861, called for all mounted regiments to be designated as cavalry and for re-numbering them as such by seniority of authorization. Thus, the

First and Second Dragoons became First and Second Cavalry, the Mounted Rifles were redesignated as the Third Cavalry and the original First and Second Cavalry regiments were changed to the Fourth and Fifth Cavalry, respectively. The original Third Cavalry which had been authorized by Congress as a new mounted regiment on July 29, 1861, was re-numbered as the Sixth U. S. Cavalry Regiment.

The original Second U. S. Cavalry Regiment had an activation span of only six years and five months — from March 3, 1855, to August 3, 1861. However, during that relatively brief period of time it made a tremendous contribution, not only to Texas and frontier history, as we have already seen, but also to American military history as well. Its horses, its equipment and its arms were the best obtainable at the time. Its private troopers appeared to be better than the average horse soldiers of that day, its noncommissioned officers were of high caliber and its officers outstanding. No other American regiment before or after has produced in so short a period of time so many general officers. Sixteen (36 per cent) of the forty-five officers that served with the Regiment while it was in Texas were promoted to General Officer rank, and "with few exceptions, the others gained field-officers' commissions." Out of the sixteen generals, eleven served in the Confederate Army and five in the Federal Army. Four of the eleven that "went South" rose to full general or four-star rank — Albert Sidney Johnston, Robert E. Lee, E. Kirby Smith and John B. Hood. Thus, the Second Cavalry furnished the Confederacy with one half of its full generals. One, William J. Hardee, was promoted to three-star or Lieutenant General status, and three, Earl Van Dorn, Charles W. Field and Fitzhugh Lee, wore the two stars of a major-general. Nathan "Shanks" Evans, J. P. Major, and G. B. Crosby became brigadier generals. Davis had stacked the cards well. The five officers who became Federal generals all attained major-general rank — George H. Thomas, Kenner Garrard, George Stoneman, Jr., Richard W. Johnson and Innis N. Palmer. It must be remembered, though that except for General U. S. Grant, no Federal general rose above two-star or major-general rank during the war.

The Second United States Cavalry was studded with stars — its sixteen generals received a total of forty-five. It would be a long time, if ever again, before America would see another regiment as elite as "Jeff Davis's Own."

INDEX

—A—

Adams, George W., 70.
Ainsworth, Gen. Miller, 13-14.
Aime, Cpl. Gustave, 76-77.
Anderson, Gen. Richard, 29.
Archer, Gen. James J., 67.
Archer, Pamela (Mrs. Audie Murphy), 10.
Arnold, Lt. A. K., 116.

—B—

Bancroft, Anne, 9.
Bass, Col. Frederick S., 25.
Bayles, Frances, 89.
Beale, Edward Fitzgerald, 49-52, 54.
Beauregard, Lt. P.G.T., 91.
Benning, Gen. Henry, 27-28.
Boteler, Col. A. R., 68.
Bottoms, Smith, 20.
Brackett, Capt. Albert G., 96, 105.
Bradfute, Capt. William, 105.
Bragg, Gen. Braxton, 41, 66, 77, 106.
Breckinridge, Gen. John C., 66.
Brewer, Theresa, 12.
Brooks, Col. Porter, 15.
Brown, Gov. Jos., 74.
Buchanan, Pres. James, 48.
Burns, Mrs. Poland (Corinne), 2, 11.
Burnside, Gen. Ambrose, 64.
Bush, Hon. George, 15.

—C—

Caan, James, 11.
Cagney, James, 9-10.
Calhoun, John C., 41, 83.
Calles, Pres. Plutarco, 56.

Camp Verde 47-49, 53-54, 114.
Camp Wolters, 3.
Campbell, Argyle, 20.
Camp Colorado, 114.
Camp Cooper, 93-94, 107-108, 110-111, 114.
Camp Hudson, 103.
Camp Radziminski, 110, 114.
Camp Sabina, 114.
Camp Van Dorn, 30.
Capps, Bolewar J., 20.
Carter, Anne Hill, 82.
Casler, John O., 67, 75.
Catton, Bruce, 22, 65, 70.
Cheatham, Gen. Benjamin F., 66.
Chimborazo Hospital, 70, 71.
Chubb, Lt. Alonzo, 69.
Clark, Roy, 12.
Coatzacoalcos, USS, 116.
Coddington, Edwin B., 71, 72.
Coffee, Lt. Col. Vernon, 15.
Colmar Pocket Campaign (WW II), 5-7.
Connally, Gov. John, 22.
Coopwood, Col. Bethal, 54.
Cortinas, Juan, 95, 96, 109.
Couch, Gen. Darius Nash, 64.
Coulter, E. Merton, 73.
Crawford, Broderick, 9.
Crittenden, Gen. George B., 66.
Crosby, Gen. G. B., 117.
Crossman, Maj. George H., 42.
Culpepper, Geo. Washington, 20.
Cunningham, H. H., 71.
Custis, G. W. P., 95.
Custis, Mary Anne Randolph, 83.

119

–D–

Darby, John F., 87.
Davis Jefferson, 32-33, 40-43, 47-48, 53, 68, 103, 117.
Dean, Jimmy, 12.
Dee, Sandra, 9.
Depfill, Capt., 55.
Donlevy, Brian, 9.
Dru, Joanna, 9.
Drumgoole, Glen, 20.

–E–

Eighteenth Ga. Inf. Regt., 19-20, 24.
Eighth U.S. Inf. Regt., 103.
Eldridge, Lt. Bolling, 34.
Elzey, Gen. Arnold, 67.
Emory, Maj. William H., 105.
Empire City, Steamer, 116.
Evans, "Buttons", 20.
Evans, Gen. Nathen G., 66, 105, 117.

–F–

Field, Gen. Charles, 28, 117.
Fifth Tex. Inf. Regt. 19, 27, 29-30, 67.
Fifteenth U.S. Inf. Regt. 3-5.
Fifth U.S. Army, 3.
Fifth U.S. Cav. Regt., 117.
Fifty-second, Indiana Inf. Regt., 71.
First Tenn. Inf. Regt., 69.
First Tex. Inf. Regt., 19, 27, 68.
First U.S. Cav. Regt., 93, 103, 105, 114, 117.
First U.S. Dragoons, 103, 116-117.
Fletcher, Bill, 31.
Floyd, John B., 48-49, 52, 96.

Ford, John, 106.
Fort Atkinson, 110.
Fort Belknap, 106-107, 109.
Fort Clark, 103, 114.
Fort George Gordon Meade, 3.
Fort Inge, 114-116.
Fort Mason, 94, 96-98, 101, 103, 107-108, 109, 113-115.
Fort McIntosh, 113.
Fort Tejon, 51-52, 54.
Fort Terrett, 101-102, 109.
Fort Washita, 106.
Forty-eighth New York Inf. Regt., 73.
Fourth Tex. Inf. Regt., 19, 23, 27, 29.
Fourth U.S. Cav. Regt., 117.
Fraser, Capt. William D., 89.
Freeman, Douglas Southall, 22, 81, 89-90, 98.
Fremantle, Lt. Col. J. A. L., 29.
Freret, Sgt. Jules, 76, 77.

–G–

Garrard, Lt. Kenner, 97, 117.
Gaston, Robert, 68.
Gleason, Jimmy, 9.
Grant, Gen. U.S., 44, 63-64, 117.
Gratiot, Gen. Chas. I, 84.
"Greek George", 55-56.
Gregg, Gen. John, 25, 28.

–H–

Hallowell, Benjamin, 82.
Hampton's Legion (Inf.), 19-20.
Hancock, Gen. Winfield S., 26-27.
Hardee, Gen. William J., 66, 94, 105, 107, 114, 117.
Hawks, Howard, 106.

INDEX

Heap, Gwinn, A., 44, 45.
Hebert, Walter, 64.
Hendrix, Wanda (Mrs. Audie Murphy), 9-10.
Hennen, Anna Maria, 24.
Hepburn, Audrey, 9.
Herr, Gen. J. K., 110.
Heth, Gen. Henry, 26.
"Hi-Jolly", 55-56.
Hill, Gen. A. P., 26-27.
Holmes, Gen. Theophilus H., 66.
Honingsberger, Ignatz, 20.
Hood, Gen. John Bell, 21, 23-24, 67, 106, 103, 109, 111, 113, 117.
Hood's Texas Brigade, 19-35, 72-73.
Hood's Texas Brigade Association, 33-34.
Hooker, Gen. Joseph, 64.
Houston, Sam, 67, 111.
Hughes, Howard, 10.
Hunt, Lt. Henry J., 84, 85.
Hutto, Reason, 20.

–I–

–J–

Jackson, Gen. Thomas J. "Stonewall", 68.
Johnson, Ben, 11.
Johnson, Capt. Richard, 97, 98, 113, 115, 117.
Johnston, Col. Albert Sidney, 93-95, 105, 107, 114, 117.
Johnston, Joseph E., 90.
Johnston, Maggie, 107.
Jones, Dick, 30.
Joskins, Joe, 67.

–K–

Kayser, Henry S., 86, 87.
Kearny, Gen. Stephen, 89.
Kennedy, Pres. John F., 15.
Kennedy, Robert, 15.
Kesselring, Field-Marshal Albert, 3.
Killian, Josie Bell, 1-2.
Kilpatrick, Gen. Judson, 65.

–L–

Ladd, Alan, 9.
Leary, William B., 82.
Lee, Robert E. IV, 22.
Lancaster, Burt, 9.
Law, Gen. Evander, 27-28.
Ledlie, Gen. James H., 65.
Lee, Lt. Fitzhugh, 111-113, 117.
Lee, George Washington Custis, 83, 86.
Lee, Gen. Henry "Light Horse Harry", 82.
Lee, Mary, 84.
Lee, Gen. Robert E., 29, 32-33, 49, 64, 72, 81-98, 105, 114-115, 117.
Lee, William Henry Fitzhugh, 84.
Lincoln, Pres. Abraham, 63, 64.
"Long Tom," 53.
Longstreet, Gen. James 27, 29.
Lord, Francis A., 64, 75.

–M–

Magruder, Gen. John, 66.
Major, Gen. J. P., 117.
Marsh, George P., 43.
Martin, Dean, 12.
Martin, Maj. William H. "Howdy", 32-33.

Mason, Chas., 83.
Massachusetts, USS., 90.
Matthau, Walter, 9.
Meade, Gen. George G., 71, 72.
Meade, Geo. Gordon, III, 22.
Meigs, Lt. Montgomery C., 84.
Meredith, Burgess, 9.
Morgan, "Mutt", 20.
Mounted Rifles, Regt., 103, 108, 114.
Murphy, Audie L., 1-16.
Murphy, Emmett Berry, 1-2.
Murphy, Skipper, 10.
Murphy, Terry, 10.

–Mc–

McArthur, Lt. J. H., 106.
McClellan, Gen. George B., 77.
McClure, "Spec", 12.
McCrea, Joel, 11.
McCulloch, Ben, 98, 105.
McDonald, Sgt. Walter, 113.
McLeneghan, Samuel, 55.
McLoughlin, John, 101.

–N–

Ninth U.S. Cav. Regt., 57.
Ninth U.S. Inf. Regt., 103.
Nolan, Lloyd, 9.

–O–

Oakes, Capt. James, 105, 108-109.
O'Hara, Capt. Theodore, 105.
Old Hutchins House (Houston), 33.
One Hundredth Ohio, Inf. Regt., 69.
One Hundredth and Tenth Penn., Inf. Regt., 76.
O'Rear, J. Pink, 20.

–P–

Palmer, Capt. I. W., 105, 116-117.
Patrick, Gen. Marsena, 72.
Pember, Phoebe, 70.
Pender, Gen. Dorsey, 21.
Perry, Eugene O., 68.
Perry, Rev. James M., 73.
Peters, Mrs. George B., 66.
Peters, Jean, 10.
Pierce, Pres. Franklin 41, 43, 48, 93.
Pillow, Gen. Gideon, 92.
Polley, J. B., 32.
Porter, Lt. David Dixon, 44-48.
Powell, Col. Robert H., 25.
Price, Gen. Sterling, 54.
Pride, Charley, 12.
Pugh, Elbert E., 20.

–Q–

–R–

Rawlins, Col. John A., 63.
Reagan, John H., 21, 33.
"Red Badge of Courage", 8-9.
Redgrave, Michael, 9.
Redwing, Rod, 11.
Reed, Donna, 9.
Reilly, Capt. James, 19.
Rhome, Romulus, T., 20.
Richardson, Rupert, 105.
Riley, Col. Bennett, 92.
Roach, "Shady," 20.
Robertson, Dale, 11.
Robertson, Gen. Jerome Bonaparte, 25, 34.
Rosser, Gen. Tom, 66.
Ryan, Capt. Ed, 30.

INDEX

–S–

Sanders, George, 9.
Santa Anna, Gen. Antonio, 90.
Scott, Gen. Winfield, 43, 88, 90, 92, 115.
Second U.S. Cav. Regt., 23, 49, 93-98, 101-117.
Second U.S. Dragoons, 103, 108, 117.
Shaaff, Lt. John T., 101.
Shannon, Fred, 70, 75.
Shannon, Sgt. Tim, 101.
Sheridan, Gen. Phil, 65.
Shields, Sen. James, 43, 92.
Shirkey, Mrs. Mary, 47.
Shropshire, Winkfield, 20.
Sibley, Gen. H. H., 65.
Sixteenth Wisc. Inf. Regt., 68, 69.
Sixth Tenn. Inf. Regt., 66.
Sixth U.S. Cav. Regt., 117.
Slocum, Gen. Henry W., 72.
Smith, Capt. E. Kirby, 105, 110, 117.
Smith, Gen. Persifor, 92.
Spangler, Sgt. John W., 110, 113.
Stacey, M. H., 49, 52.
Stalcup, Jasper, 20.
Steincipher, John, 20.
Stevens, John, 32.
Stewart, James, 9.
Stoneman, Capt. George, Jr., 105, 109, 117.
Stonewall Brigade, 67, 75.
Supply, USS, 44-47.

–T–

Taylor, Gen. Zachary, 40, 88-89.
Tedro, Phillip, 56.
Tenth U.S. Inf. Regt., 103.
"The Unforgiven", 9.
Thirty-Sixth U.S. Inf. Div., 13-14.
Third, Ark., Inf. Regt., 27-28.
Third U.S. Cav. Regt., 113, 117.
Third U.S. Inf. Div., 3.
Thomas, Maj. George H., 49, 101, 105, 109-111, 114, 117.
Tibbs, Casey, 11.
Tilly, Ed, 30.
"To Hell And Back", 9, 12.
Totten, Gen. James, 64-65.
"Traveller", 27.
Travis, Capt. Charles, 105.
Travis, Col. William Barrett, 105.
Turner, Scott, 12.
Twelfth U.S. Corps, 72.
Twenty-First-Ill; Inf. Regt., 7, 63.
Twiggs, Gen. David E., 92, 95-97, 110, 115.

–U–

–V–

Van Camp, Lt. Cornelius, 110.
Van Dorn, Gen. Earl, 66, 105, 109-111, 113, 114-115, 117.
Venable, Col. Charles, 27.
Villepique, Gen. John B., 66.

–W–

Wallace, Jerry, 12.
Walsh, Raoul, 106.
Watkins, Pvt. Sam, 69.
Wayne, Maj. Henry C., 42, 44-45, 47-48, 52.

Westmoreland, Gen. Wm. C., 15.
Whiting, Capt. Chas. J., 67, 105.
Wigfall, Louis T., 21-23, 67, 68.
Wilcox, Gen. Cadmus M., 26.
Wiley, Bell I., 62, 73-74.
Williams, Ben Ames, 22.
Winkler, Col. C. M., 25, 34.
Witherall, Lt. James B., 110.

Wofford, Col. William T., 24.
Wollard, Andy, 30.
Wolseley, Col. Garnet J., 21, 29.
Wood, Lt. Robt. C., Jr., 105, 111.
Wool, Gen. John E., 88, 89.
Worth, Gen. William J., 89.
Wyatt, Jane, 9.

–XYZ–